MY WELLBEING

JOURNEY

1

SECOND EDITION

JUNIOR CYCLE SPHE

EDEL O'BRIEN

 GILL EDUCATION

Gill Education
Hume Avenue
Park West
Dublin 12
www.gilleducation.ie

Gill Education is an imprint of M.H. Gill & Co.

ISBN: 978-0-7171-99723

Design: Síofra Murphy
Illustrations: Derry Dillon and Andrii Yankovskyi

At the time of going to press, all web addresses were active and contained information relevant to the topics in this book. Gill Education does not, however, accept responsibility for the content or views contained on these websites. Content, views and addresses may change beyond the publisher or author's control. Students should always be supervised when reviewing websites.

For permission to reproduce photographs, the authors and publisher gratefully acknowledge the following:

© Adobe Stock: 12, 13, 16, 17, 23, 24, 31, 34, 35, 39, 42, 45, 47, 49, 51, 72TL, 72CR, 87, 89, 93T, 97, 98, 100, 111, 112, 112L, 115, 125T, 126, 127, 132, 137, 139L, 140, 141, 146, 147, 155, 158, 159, 162, 164, 165, 167, 168, 170, 174, 177, 182, 190, 191TR, 191BL, 199, 202, 203, 205, 206, 220; © Alamy: 9T, 9BC, 84, 192C, 192B; © BodyWhys.ie: 150a; © Getty Images: 93B, 223; © Hotline.ie: 150j; © Irish Heart Foundation: 193L; © Irish Society for the Prevention of Cruelty to Children (ISPCC): 150f, 150h; © iStock/Getty Premium: 2, 9TC, 9B, 10, 12, 23, 43, 54, 69, 72TR, 72C, 72CL, 72B, 81, 92, 93TC, 93BC, 102, 112R, 115CBR, 135, 139R, 143T, 143TC, 143BC, 157, 190CL, 191TL, 191BR, 215; © Rainbows Ireland: 150m; © Shutterstock: 65, 193R, 143B, 143T, 225; © St Vincent de Paul: 150g; © Text About it: 150k; © Webwise.ie: 150c.

The authors and publisher have made every effort to trace all copyright holders. If, however, any have been inadvertently overlooked, we would be pleased to make the necessary arrangement at the first opportunity.

CONTENTS

Scan the QR code to access an additional lesson on Kindness on GillExplore.ie.

Introduction to *My Wellbeing Journey 1*

Welcome to Junior Cycle Social, Personal and Health Education (SPHE)! This is a subject that is unlike nearly any other subject you will take for the Junior Cycle. There is no final exam. Instead, the focus of the subject is on you and your health and wellbeing!

This is an especially exciting time to be taking SPHE, as the course has been revised so that it better prepares you for the challenges of the fast-changing modern world. The course is based on respect, equality, responsibility, dignity, compassion and empathy and is inclusive of all.

Notably, the Relationships and Sexuality Education (RSE) strand of the course has been updated for the first time in 20 years. RSE is a key part of SPHE and provides a safe space for you to think about and discuss relationships, sexuality, healthy sexual expression and reproductive health. The purpose of the RSE lessons is very much in line with the rest of the course: to support you in living safe, happy, fulfilling lives.

SPHE gives you the chance to develop a strong sense of self and to gain the life skills and knowledge required. You'll learn to make informed decisions about health and wellbeing, you will develop the resilience needed to support emotional wellbeing and you will learn to be empathetic and nurture respectful, loving relationships and contribute positively to society.

SPHE supports each of the six indicators of Wellbeing:

 active responsible connected resilient respected aware

For that reason, SPHE and *My Wellbeing Journey* contributes significantly to your school's Wellbeing programme.

SPHE and *My Wellbeing Journey* put you at the centre of the learning experience. The active learning methods used throughout this series encourage you to engage fully with the topics discussed. We hope that the activities presented in *My Wellbeing Journey* will make for fun, thought-provoking and valuable SPHE classes.

Edel O'Brien

Using *My Wellbeing Journey 1*

Specification Links

My Wellbeing Journey is clearly linked to the SPHE specification. Each year is broken into six units of learning and 33 hour-long lessons. At the start of each lesson, the relevant Learning Outcomes and Wellbeing Indicators are clearly highlighted. Learning Outcomes are then broken down further into student-friendly learning intentions. This very clear curriculum mapping will support planning.

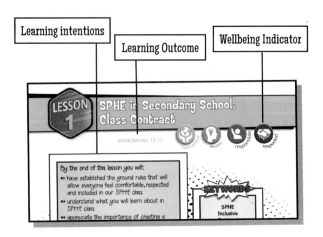

Support

Throughout the lessons, recommended Additional Resources are clearly highlighted to support further exploration of topics and to highlight where help can be found, if needed. We also provide significant support for the teaching of these lessons with PowerPoints provided for every lesson. PowerPoint icons are included throughout the book whenever significant additional material is provided within the PowerPoints.

Reflection

Reflecting on learning is an important aspect of the Junior Cycle Framework. The Reflections at the end of each lesson provide scaffolding for regular reflection. These reflections are particularly useful when it comes to preparing a CBA in 2nd or 3rd Year and for supporting communication with parents.

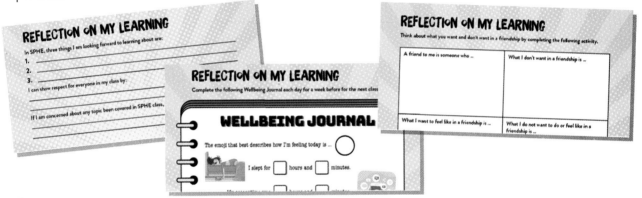

Assessment

The focal point for assessment in SPHE is the Classroom-Based Assessment, which can be carried out in either 2nd or 3rd Year. You have two options for the CBA. You can compile a portfolio of learning and reflections, which comprises three different pieces of work, each linked to different strands of learning. Alternatively you can carry out an action project to raise awareness or promote an aspect of health and wellbeing studied. This book includes some CBA suggestions; more ideas and guidance are provided in Books 2 and 3.

Additional Resources

Countless other resources, which support teaching and learning in SPHE, are included on GillExplore.ie. They include PowerPoints, videos, editable planning materials and additional optional lessons, as well as the *My Wellbeing Journey Teacher's Resource Book*.

Using *My Wellbeing Journey* to Meet JC SPHE and Wellbeing Requirements

All students at Junior Cycle must have 400 hours of wellbeing-related learning across the three years. SPHE must be taught for 100 of these hours, with students having SPHE classes in each of the three years. From September 2023, it is compulsory that 1st Year students follow the newly developed SPHE specification. The updated editions of *My Wellbeing Journey* cover all SPHE requirements, in ready-to-use lessons, which are carefully scaffolded and have been tested robustly.

How *My Wellbeing Journey* Helps you Fulfil the Learning Outcomes of the SPHE Course

The table below highlights where the various Learning Outcomes from the SPHE specification are addressed in this book. Because of the spiral nature of the course, many of the Learning Outcomes are revisited again across lessons in Books 2 and 3. Some Learning Outcomes aren't covered until Books 2 and 3 to ensure that learning has been properly scaffolded and to ensure that students have the maturity to access the content in a meaningful way.

Strand 1: Understanding Myself and Others

Students should be able to:	Relevant lessons
1.1 explore the physical, social and emotional changes that happen during adolescence	Lessons 17, 18
1.2 reflect on their personal strengths and values and how they bring these into relationships	Lessons 4, 22
1.3 explore the range of influences and life experiences that can impact on self-image and self-esteem and identify ways to nurture a positive sense of self-worth	Lesson 5
1.4 recognise the factors and influences that shape young people's self-identity, such as family, peers, culture, gender identity, sexual orientation, race/ethnic background, dis/abilities, religious beliefs/world-views	Lessons 5, 20, 21
1.5 reflect on gender equity and how gender stereotypes impact on expectations, behaviour and relationships	Lessons 19, 20, 29
1.6 discuss experiences/situations of bias, inequality or exclusion and devise ways to actively create more inclusive environments	Lessons 1, 19, 20
1.7 communicate in a respectful and effective manner and listen openly and sensitively to the views/feelings of others	Lessons 1, 2, 7, 12, 13, 14, 16, 20, 22
1.8 reflect on the meaning and importance of empathy and discuss ways that it can be expressed	Lesson 7
1.9 demonstrate self-management skills, including setting personal goals, delaying gratification, and self-regulation of thoughts, emotions and impulses.	Lessons 6, 24, 25, 26

Strand 2: Making Healthy Choices

Students should be able to:	Relevant lessons
2.1 consider the multifaceted nature of health and wellbeing, and evaluate what being healthy might look like for different adolescents, including how food, physical activity, sleep/rest and hygiene contribute to health and wellbeing	Lessons 3, 27, 28, 29, 30
2.2 investigate how unhealthy products such as nicotine, vapes, alcohol, and unhealthy food and drinks are marketed and advertised	Lessons 28, 33
2.3 discuss societal, cultural and economic influences affecting young people when it comes to making healthy choices about smoking, alcohol and other addictive substances and behaviours, and how harmful influences can be overcome in real-life situations	Lesson 33
2.4 demonstrate skills and strategies to help make informed choices that support health and wellbeing and apply them in real-life situations that may be stressful and/or involve difficult peer situations	Lessons 27, 33
2.5 discuss the physical, social, emotional and legal consequences of using addictive substances – immediate and long-term	Lessons 31, 32, 33
2.6 consider scenarios where, for example, alcohol, nicotine, drugs, food and electronic devices might be used to cope with unpleasant feelings or stress, and discuss possible healthy ways of coping	Lessons 26, 33
2.7 assess the benefits and difficulties associated with their online world and discuss strategies for dealing with a range of scenarios that might arise	Lessons 15, 26
2.8 discuss how to share personal information, images, opinions and emotions in a safe, responsible and respectful manner online and in person	Lesson 15
2.9 explore why young people share sexual imagery online and examine the risks and consequences of doing this	Lesson 15
2.10 demonstrate how to access and appraise appropriate and trustworthy information, supports and services about health and wellbeing.	See *My Wellbeing Journey 2*

Strand 3: Relationships and Sexuality

Students should be able to:	Relevant lessons
3.1 reflect on the values, behaviours and skills that help to make, sustain and end relationships respectfully with friends, family and romantic/intimate relationships	Lessons 2, 8, 22
3.2 examine benefits and difficulties experienced by young people in a range of relationships – friendships, family relationships, and romantic/intimate relationships	Lessons 2, 22
3.3 identify signs of healthy, unhealthy and abusive relationships	See *My Wellbeing Journey 2*
3.4 appreciate the importance of setting healthy boundaries in relationships and consider how to show respect for the boundaries of others	Lesson 22
3.5 consider the importance of taking care of their reproductive health	Lessons 17, 18
3.6 appreciate the breadth of what constitutes human sexuality, and how sexual orientation and gender identity are experienced and expressed in diverse ways	Lessons 16, 20, 21
3.7 explore the pressures to become sexually intimate and discuss ways to show respect for people's choices	See *My Wellbeing Journey 3*
3.8 appreciate the importance of seeking, giving and receiving consent in sexual relationships, from the perspective of building caring relationships and from a legal perspective	See *My Wellbeing Journey 2*
3.9 explain the importance of safer sexual activity with reference to methods of contraception and protection against sexually transmitted infections (STIs)	See *My Wellbeing Journey 3*
3.10 discuss the influence of popular culture and the online world, in particular, the influence of pornography, on young people's understanding, expectations and social norms in relation to sexual expression	See *My Wellbeing Journey 2*
3.11 demonstrate how to access and appraise appropriate and trustworthy advice, support and services related to relationships and sexual health.	See *My Wellbeing Journey 2*

Strand 4: Emotional Wellbeing

Students should be able to:	Relevant lessons
4.1 discuss the fluid nature of emotional wellbeing and ways to nurture and protect it	Lessons 3, 23, 24, 25
4.2 recognise and acknowledge their emotions and recognise the links between thoughts, feelings and behaviour	Lessons 7, 24, 25
4.3 consider the impact of stress and draw upon a variety of techniques to help self-regulate emotions and cope with the day-to-day stresses of life	Lesson 24
4.4 discuss ways to support themselves and others in challenging times and where/how/when to seek support, if needed	Lessons 2, 8, 9, 10, 11, 23, 24, 25
4.5 explore how emotional wellbeing can be affected by factors within our control, such as sleep, diet, exercise, substance use and online exposure, and factors beyond our control	Lessons 3, 26
4.6 recognise different kinds of abusive and bullying behaviour that can occur in interactions online and in person	Lessons 9, 11
4.7 explain why noticing and responding to different kinds of abusive or bullying behaviour that can occur in person and online is important and discuss appropriate responses, including, why, how, where and when to report	Lessons 9, 11, 21
4.8 identify actions young people can take, without putting themselves at risk, in situations where they are aware of incidents of abusive behaviour or bullying happening and explore the barriers to standing up	Lessons 10, 11, 21
4.9 demonstrate how to access and appraise appropriate and trustworthy information and services aimed at supporting young people's emotional wellbeing and mental health.	See *My Wellbeing Journey 2*

UNIT 1

UNDERSTANDING MYSELF AND OTHERS

Scan the QR code to access an additional lesson on Kindness on GillExplore.ie.

LESSON 1
SPHE in Secondary School: Class Contract

Learning Outcomes: 1.6, 1.7

connected   aware   responsible   respected

By the end of this lesson, you will:

→ have established the ground rules that will allow everyone to feel comfortable, respected and included in our SPHE class

→ understand what you will learn about in SPHE class

→ appreciate the importance of creating a classroom environment where everyone feels safe and respected.

KEYWORDS

SPHE
Inclusive
Contract
Confidentiality

ADDITIONAL RESOURCES

www.childline.ie Childline is a 24-hour helpline and online service that offers advice and support to children and young people under 18. **Freephone 1800 666 666.**

Text 50808 A free, anonymous 24-hour messaging service that provides everything from a calming chat to immediate support. This text service is a safe space where you are listened to by a trained volunteer. By asking questions, listening to you and responding with support, they will help you sort through your feelings until you both feel you are now in a calm, safe place.

www.kidshealth.org The teen section of this website provides support and advice for teenagers on health and wellbeing and different aspects of teenage life.

Overview of SPHE

SPHE in secondary school will help you develop a positive sense of yourself and will give you the skills for caring for yourself and others. It will help you make good choices about your own health and wellbeing and help you cope with the challenges that come with the teenage years. You will probably remember doing SPHE in primary school.

GROUP ACTIVITY

What do you remember from your SPHE classes in primary school? In groups, discuss what you learned about in SPHE and why it is important in your life, then write your ideas on the notes below.

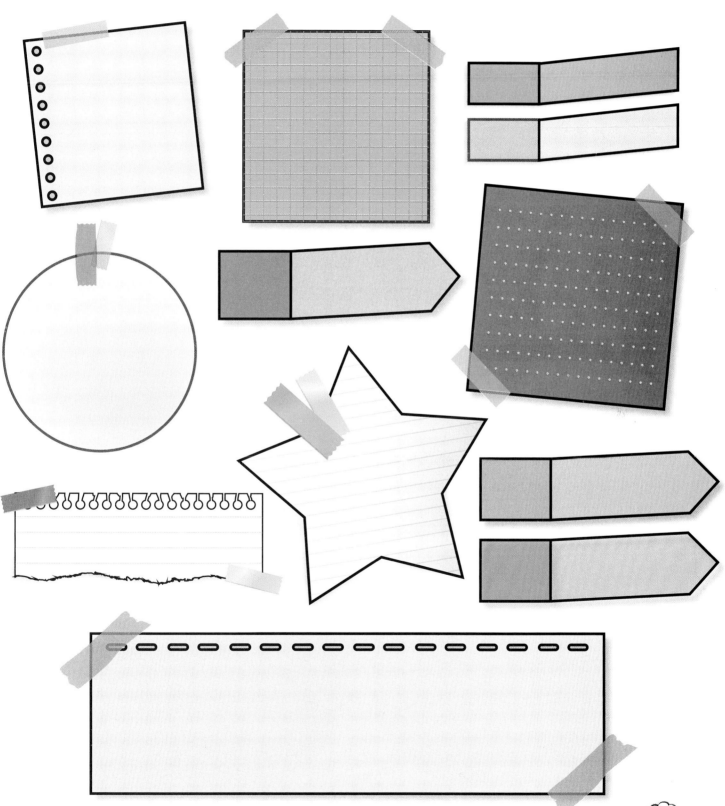

SPHE in Secondary School

SPHE in secondary school aims to build upon what you learned in primary school. Here is an overview of what you will learn in SPHE class over the next three years of Junior Cycle:

Strand 1: Understanding Myself and Others

In this strand, you will learn about:

- being an adolescent and the challenges of teenage years
- building your own self-esteem, self-identity and self-worth
- what shapes the person you are
- gender stereotypes and gender equity
- respecting difference
- how to show and express empathy
- self-management (goal setting)
- regulating your emotions
- respectful communication.

Strand 2: Making Healthy Choices

In this strand, you will learn about:

- what it means to be healthy
- how diet, physical activity, sleep/rest and hygiene contribute to health and wellbeing
- substance misuse (addictive substances)
- staying safe online
- sexting
- how to access trustworthy supports about health and wellbeing.

Strand 4: Emotional Wellbeing

In this strand, you will learn about:

- how to nurture your emotional wellbeing
- how to cope with the normal emotional ups and downs of teenage life
- developing coping skills to deal with tough times
- how to find support in challenging times
- how our thoughts, feelings and behaviours are linked
- how to deal with and respond to bullying situations
- how to access trustworthy information and services aimed at supporting young people's emotional wellbeing and mental health.

Strand 3: Relationships and Sexuality

In this strand, you will learn about:

- how to create and maintain healthy and respectful relationships
- relationship difficulties experienced by young people
- healthy, unhealthy and abusive relationships
- the importance of consent in relationships
- how to set boundaries and respect others' boundaries
- how to take care of your reproductive health
- sexuality
- online influence on relationships
- how to access trustworthy supports about sexual health and relationships, and information related to relationships and sexual health.

CLASS DISCUSSION

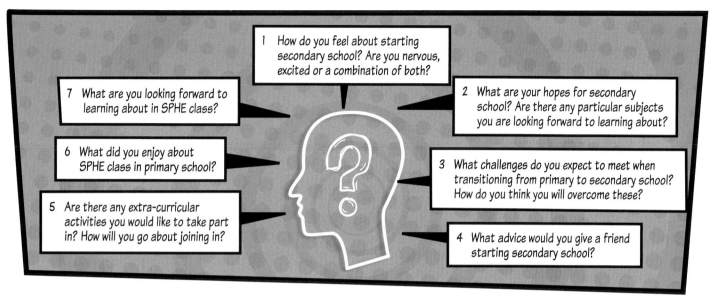

1 How do you feel about starting secondary school? Are you nervous, excited or a combination of both?

2 What are your hopes for secondary school? Are there any particular subjects you are looking forward to learning about?

3 What challenges do you expect to meet when transitioning from primary to secondary school? How do you think you will overcome these?

4 What advice would you give a friend starting secondary school?

5 Are there any extra-curricular activities you would like to take part in? How will you go about joining in?

6 What did you enjoy about SPHE class in primary school?

7 What are you looking forward to learning about in SPHE class?

For the SPHE class to work well together, we need to have a number of ground rules to ensure that everyone feels safe, respected and included in class. Sometimes in SPHE class, we will be discussing sensitive topics. For this reason, confidentiality is very important. We need to respect our own privacy and the privacy of others. Some things are personal and it may not be appropriate to talk about them in class discussions. It is important that we don't use names or descriptions that would identify others.

Limits of Confidentiality

Remember: If you reveal something in class that your teacher believes puts you or another student at risk of harm, your teacher must report this to keep you safe. If you feel concerned or sensitive about certain things, it is important to speak to a trusted adult.

INDIVIDUAL ACTIVITY

Confidentiality – respecting the privacy of others and keeping private what they say in class – is one of the most important ground rules for SPHE class. There are other important ground rules, for example:

1. Listening while others are speaking.
2. Respecting other people's opinions.

Add what you think might be three other important ground rules for participating in SPHE class.

3. _____

4. _____

5. _____

GROUP ACTIVITY

Now share your ground rules in groups of three or four. As a group, decide on the five ground rules you consider to be the most important. When you have decided on the top five rules, fill in the placards. Nominate a **reporter** to give feedback from your group to the teacher.

A REPORTER is the person who gives feedback to the teacher/to the class on behalf of the group.

CLASS ACTIVITY

The whole class must now agree on a set of ground rules. Ensure each ground rule begins with an 'I' statement, e.g. 'I will listen when others are speaking.' When agreement has been reached on these ground rules, write them into the contract. Everyone must sign their own contract to show that they agree.

CLASS CONTRACT

Signed:

REFLECTION ON MY LEARNING

In SPHE, three things I am looking forward to learning about are:

1. _____

2. _____

3. _____

I can show respect for everyone in my class by:

_____

_____

If I am concerned about any topic being covered in SPHE class, I can:

_____

_____

LESSON 2

Joining a New Group

Learning Outcomes: 1.7, 3.1, 4.4

respected resilient connected responsible

By the end of this lesson, you will:

- get to know people in your class better
- understand the challenges that come with starting secondary school
- identify ways to make and maintain friendships
- be aware of where to get help or what you can do if you have any concerns.

KEYWORDS

Friendships
Challenges
Concerns

ADDITIONAL RESOURCES

www.childline.ie Childline is a 24-hour helpline and online service that offers advice and support to children and young people under 18. **Freephone 1800 666 666.**

CLASS ACTIVITY

- You have 15 minutes to walk around the classroom and meet as many students as possible, and to ask them a question from the table below.
- Fill in their name and their answer.
- You cannot answer the same question twice!
- When the time is up, return to your seat and read over the answers.
- Highlight any answers you really like.

Name	Question	Answer
	If you could travel back in time, what period of history would you go back to?	
	What country would you really like to visit?	
	If you could watch any movie right now, what would it be?	
	What famous person in the world would you most like to spend a day with?	
	If you don't have a pet, what sort of pet would you like to have? If you do, what sort of pet do you have and what is its name?	
	If you were an animal, which animal would you be?	
	What is your favourite thing to do in the summer?	
	What is your favourite day of the week?	
	If you were going to be marooned on a desert island, what three things would you bring with you?	
	If you won the lotto, what would you do with the money?	
	Who is your favourite cartoon or comic book character?	
	Were you named after someone special? If so, who?	
	What is your favourite TV programme?	
	What is your favourite book?	
	What is the weirdest thing you have ever eaten?	
	How tall are you?	
	What is the hardest thing you have ever done?	

Go to next page ... →

	If you were at a friend's house and found an insect in your dinner, what would you do?	
	Do you prefer Italian food or Chinese food?	
	If you could change one thing in the world, what would it be?	
	Would you most like to be happy, or rich, or famous?	
	Can you sing or play a musical instrument? 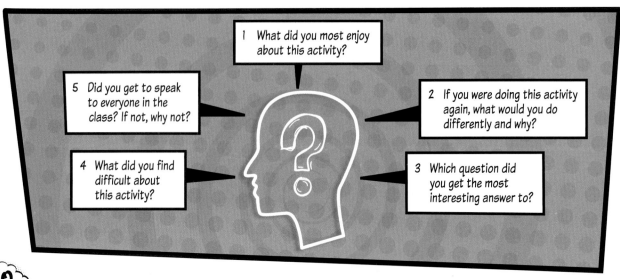	
	Who is your hero and why?	
	What is the funniest thing that has ever happened to you?	
	Would you rather be too hungry or too cold?	
	Would you prefer to sleep in the top bunk or the bottom bunk?	
	If you could change your first name, what would you change it to?	

CLASS DISCUSSION

1 What did you most enjoy about this activity?

5 Did you get to speak to everyone in the class? If not, why not?

2 If you were doing this activity again, what would you do differently and why?

4 What did you find difficult about this activity?

3 Which question did you get the most interesting answer to?

Moving from Primary School to Secondary School

Moving up to secondary school is the start of a new chapter in your life. This can be an exciting and nervous time. A new school brings with it a lot of changes – new teachers, new subjects, a new timetable, new classmates, a new building. You may feel a little apprehensive about settling in. This is all very natural, and everyone will be in the same boat. The following quiz will help you cope with the exciting changes you will come across as you settle into secondary school.

INDIVIDUAL ACTIVITY

Starting Secondary School Quiz

What are you looking forward to in secondary school?

What are your main concerns about starting secondary school?

What would help you settle into secondary school?

I can show respect for others by …

I can be organised and prepared in school by …

What could you do to make and maintain friendships?

I can get organised and prepared for school the night before by …

Who's who?

Principal _____

Deputy principal/s _____

Year head _____

Class tutor _____

Guidance counsellor _____

Caretaker _____

Secretary _____

How can you support others starting secondary school?

Who can support you starting secondary school?

Who can you talk to if you have any questions?

A question I still have is:

Making Friends

Starting secondary school is a great opportunity to make lifelong friends and build on the friendships you now have. People have different experiences when starting secondary school. Some students may have lots of friends from primary school while others may not know anyone. In small groups, read the following and answer the questions.

1. Sarah is starting secondary school, but none of her friends from primary school are in her new school.
   - Why might this be a good thing?

   _____

   _____

   - What might be challenging about this situation?

   _____

   _____

   - What advice would you give Sarah?

   _____

   _____

2. Mohammed is starting secondary school. Three of his best friends from primary school are in his class.
   - Why might this be a good thing?

   _____

   _____

   - What might be challenging about this situation?

   _____

   _____

   - What advice would you give Mohammed?

   _____

   _____

3. Gena's dad had to change jobs, so she had to start secondary school in a new country.
   - What might be challenging about this situation?

   _____

   _____

   - What advice would you give Gena?

   _____

   _____

REFLECTION ON MY LEARNING

My hopes for secondary school are:

_____

_____

I can make this happen by:

_____

_____

I can offer support to others by:

_____

_____

I can receive support by:

_____

_____

LESSON 3

Understanding Wellbeing

Learning Outcomes: 2.1, 4.1, 4.5

By the end of this lesson, you will:
- understand what wellbeing means
- identify a range of ways to promote your wellbeing
- evaluate what is most effective in supporting your own wellbeing.

KEYWORDS

Wellbeing
Wellbeing indicators

ADDITIONAL RESOURCES

www.jigsaw.ie Provides information and advice on a range of issues faced by young people.

www.barnardos.ie/teenhelp Search the 'finding help' section for contact details of organisations, websites and helplines that provide information, advice and support for young people.

www.walkinmyshoes.ie Walk in My Shoes is a mental health awareness campaign developed by St Patrick's Mental Health Services. Its website provides resources for young people, such as the Wellbeing Action Calendar, Wellness Journals and Mindful Colouring Sheets.

What is Wellbeing?

We hear the word 'wellbeing' a lot in our daily lives – but what does it mean to experience wellbeing? Wellbeing is present when:

- we are aware of what we want and what we are good at
- we eat well, and get enough exercise and sleep
- we feel we belong or are part of a group or the wider community
- we can manage problems or stresses that are part of life
- we enjoy learning new things

We all experience ups and downs, but our wellbeing is central to our lives. The six indicators of wellbeing – Active, Responsible, Connected, Resilient, Respected and Aware – describe what young people need to be 'well'.

14

ACTIVE
★ Am I a confident and skilled participant in physical activity?
★ How physically active am I?

CONNECTED
★ Do I feel connected to my school, my friends, my community and the wider world?
★ Do I appreciate that my actions and interactions impact on my own wellbeing and that of others, in local and global contexts?

RESPECTED
★ Do I feel that I am listened to and valued?
★ Do I have positive relationships with my friends, my peers and my teachers?
★ Do I show care and respect for others?

INDICATORS OF WELLBEING

 active responsible connected resilient respected aware

RESPONSIBLE
★ Do I take action to protect and promote my wellbeing and that of others?
★ Do I make healthy eating choices?
★ Do I know when my safety is at risk and do I make right choices?

RESILIENT
★ Do I believe that I have the coping skills to deal with life's challenges?
★ Do I know where I can go for help?
★ Do I believe that with effort I can achieve?

AWARE
★ Am I aware of my thoughts, feelings and behaviours and can I make sense of them?
★ Am I aware of what my personal values are and do I think through my decisions?
★ Do I understand what helps me to learn and how I can improve?

GROUP ACTIVITY

Find Someone Who: Wellbeing Walkabout

You will have many opportunities to mind your wellbeing every day. The following activity shows different ways people your age can look after their wellbeing.

- You have 10 minutes to walk around the classroom.
- Find someone who does an activity in the grid.
- Fill in their name.
- You cannot answer the same question twice!

eats five or more portions of fruit and veg per day	tried a new activity or hobby recently	practises relaxation or mindfulness	is learning something new	baked or cooked something new
gets a good night's sleep most nights	joined a new group or club	did something nice for a friend	likes going on nature walks or walking on the beach	complimented someone recently
has a healthy lunch	keeps active	turns off their phone before going to bed	has an interesting hobby	puts their phone away in company
finds joy in music	drinks eight glasses of water a day	did something kind for a stranger	talks to someone if they are worried	enjoys reading
spends time with friends	made a mistake but learned from it	wrote a card or letter to thank someone	spends time with family	writes down what they are grateful for
volunteers	watched something funny	thanked a friend	made a list of their positive qualities	likes spending time with their pet

CLASS DISCUSSION

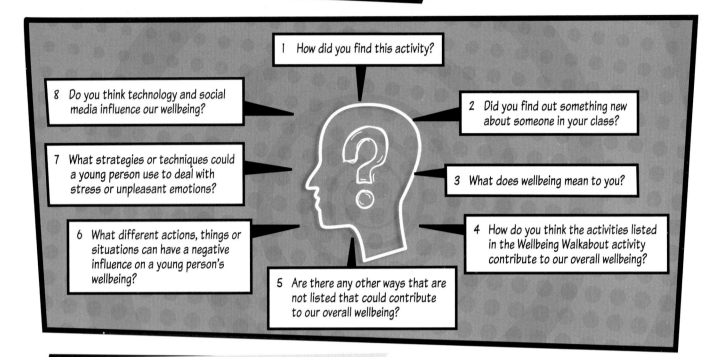

1 How did you find this activity?

8 Do you think technology and social media influence our wellbeing?

2 Did you find out something new about someone in your class?

7 What strategies or techniques could a young person use to deal with stress or unpleasant emotions?

3 What does wellbeing mean to you?

6 What different actions, things or situations can have a negative influence on a young person's wellbeing?

4 How do you think the activities listed in the Wellbeing Walkabout activity contribute to our overall wellbeing?

5 Are there any other ways that are not listed that could contribute to our overall wellbeing?

INDIVIDUAL ACTIVITY

Read the story below and make a list of activities or experiences that may have a positive or negative effect on Jack's wellbeing. Think about the following:

- Jack's phone use
- his diet and exercise habits
- his sleep patterns
- his interactions with friends, family and teachers
- his time management and organisation.

A DAY IN THE LIFE OF JACK

It's 7.30 a.m. – Jack's mobile phone alarm goes off. He is feeling tired, as he stayed up late playing his favourite online game. He reaches for his phone and begins scrolling through his messages and social media. He doesn't feel the time passing, and at 8.00 a.m. he hears his mother calling from downstairs to get up or he will be late. He finally gets up at 8.30 a.m. He doesn't have time for a shower now. He gets dressed in a hurry. He can't find his tie, so he decides he will have to do without it and runs downstairs.

Jack meets his mother in the kitchen and tells her he doesn't have time for breakfast. He asks his mother for money for a school trip and for sausage rolls on the way to school. His mother is annoyed that he is late and that he hasn't told her about the trip sooner. Jack feels bad about upsetting her, as he knows she has a lot on with his granny sick in the hospital. She says she will transfer the money to him online. He leaves the house and meets his friend Con at the corner. They walk to school. On the way to school, they laugh and joke about the day before and the soccer game. Jack tells Con he had a great game.

Jack arrives at school at 9.05 a.m., but school started at 9.00 a.m. He meets the principal at the door, who gives him two notes – one for not having a tie and one for being late. Jack makes his way to his Geography class, which is his favourite subject. During the class, his teacher praises him for making an excellent poster on volcanoes.

At 10.00 a.m., Jack is in Science class. He is feeling hungry and has an hour to go until breaktime. He is distracted and doesn't pay much attention to the lesson. Breaktime is at 11.00 a.m. Jack rushes to copy his friend's Maths homework, as he didn't get time to complete it last night, having spent too much time on his Geography poster. He has a sausage roll from this morning, so he quickly eats that. After break, Jack has PE class. He loves PE, so he is raging because in all his rushing this morning, he has forgotten his PE gear. He gets a note from his PE teacher.

Lunch is at 1.00 p.m. Jack meets with his friends in the yard. He is delighted as he made his lunch the night before – mixed fruit, chicken pasta and a yoghurt.

Jack's last classes are Art and Maths. He enjoys Art class, as he is quite good at it. He is very tired in Maths class and finds it difficult to concentrate.

After school, he waits for Con, and they walk home together. On the way home, they take the time to check their phones, scrolling through social media, checking posts and sending snaps to friends. They decide to stop in the local shop and Jack decides to get crisps, sweets and an energy drink, as he has a soccer match later and he feels he will need the energy.

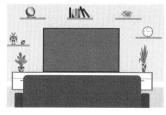

Jack arrives home at 4.15 p.m. and is greeted enthusiastically at the door by his dog, Jeff. He watches TV for an hour, while scrolling on his phone. He clears out the dishwasher for his parents and tidies around. He has a soccer match at 7.00 p.m., so he decides to start his homework. He completes Geography first, as this is his favourite subject. While doing his homework, he keeps getting distracted by his phone.

Jack's dad arrives home at 6.00 p.m. and makes dinner. Jack eats his dinner in front of the TV while finishing his homework, but he isn't that hungry after the sweets, so he leaves most of it. He gets ready for his match and his father drops him to the pitch.

In the second half of the game, Jack's coach calls him to the side line. He is disappointed, but he speaks to his dad about it in the car on the way home, and his dad makes him feel better about it.

Jack arrives home at 9.00 p.m. His parents praise him for helping out with the housework. He wants to be more organised for tomorrow, so he packs his lunch and gets his bag ready for the morning. He goes to bed at 11.00 p.m. He reads a few chapters of his favourite book until he is tired and then falls asleep.

Positive effects on Jack's wellbeing 👍	Negative effects on Jack's wellbeing 👎

What Jack could have done differently to support his wellbeing

INDIVIDUAL ACTIVITY

Supporting My Own Wellbeing

Scattered around the hand below are different activities and techniques that we can use to support our wellbeing.

On the fingers of the hand, write the top five things that contribute to your wellbeing. On the palm of the hand, write any other activities you could do to promote your wellbeing. You can add your own or just use the ones provided.

Talking about how you feel with others

Practising relaxation techniques such as mindfulness

Volunteering in the community

Taking time out to rest and unwind

Exercise

Spending time with friends and family

Eating healthily

Getting enough sleep

Writing your feelings in a journal or diary

Learning new things

Listening to music

Using humour to improve your mood

Thinking positive thoughts

Taking time out and coming back to a problem later

Doing absorbing activities like crosswords or puzzles

Walking the dog

REFLECTION ON MY LEARNING

Complete the following Wellbeing Journal each day for a week before for the next class.

WELLBEING JOURNAL

The emoji that best describes how I'm feeling today is ... ◯

I slept for ☐ hours and ☐ minutes.

My screen time was ☐ hours and ☐ minutes.

I drank ☐ glasses of water.

I ate ☐ servings of fruit and veg.

My physical activity today was _____.

Three things I am grateful for today are:

1. _____

2. _____

3. _____

Two things I am doing well to support my wellbeing:

★ _____

★ _____

One thing I need to improve on to support my wellbeing:

_____

Someone who I can talk to about my wellbeing:

_____

LESSON 4

Understanding Myself: My Strengths

Learning Outcome: 1.2

resilient   respected   connected   responsible

By the end of this lesson, you will:

→ have reflected on your personal strengths
→ identified how you demonstrate your strengths in different aspects of your life
→ appreciate the strengths of others.

KEYWORDS

Self-esteem
Self-worth
Personal strengths
Compliments

ADDITIONAL RESOURCES

www.childline.ie Childline is a 24-hour helpline and online service that offers advice and support to children and young people under 18. **Freephone 1800 666 666.**

Text 50808 A free, anonymous 24-hour messaging service that provides everything from a calming chat to immediate support. This text service is a safe space where you are listened to by a trained volunteer. By asking questions, listening to you and responding with support, they will help you sort through your feelings until you are in a calm, safe place.

www.kidshealth.org The teen section of this website provides support and advice for teenagers on health and wellbeing and different aspects of teenage life.

Personal Strengths

We all have unique personal strengths. These are the special qualities and abilities that make us uniqu, the ones others see in us when they get to know us and often the qualities we value in others. Examples of strengthsare showing kindness, showing bravery or being creative.

It can be difficult sometimes to recognise our own strengths, but identifying our strengths is vital to promoting positive health and wellbeing. It helps to build our self-esteem and self-worth, discover what's important to us, and achieve our goals.

It is only by learning to appreciate ourselves that we can really begin to appreciate others in our lives. In this lesson, you will reflect on your own personal strengths. Use the different examples of personal strengths below to help you complete the next activity.

Self-esteem: How much you value yourself as a person. Having a healthy self-esteem means you feel good about yourself, believe in yourself and are proud of your achievements.

Self-image: How you see yourself. Having a positive self-image means recognising your strengths, talents and abilities, but also recognising where you can improve. Having a positive self-image means appreciating and accepting yourself for who you are.

Enthusiasm
I take on each day with energy and excitement

Friendship
I get along well with others and my friends can count on me

Gratitude
I appreciate the good things that happen to me and that others do for me

Perseverance
I work hard to achieve my goals and don't give up!

Creativity
I can use my imagination to solve problems and enjoy life

Curiosity
I explore the world around me and have fun learning

Love of learning
I love discovering new things

Humour
I like to make people laugh and smile

Bravery
I take on challenges and speak up for what's right

Optimism
I always think the best of things and of people

Self-control
I can manage my emotions and not blow up at people

Kindness
I am helpful and nice to others

Appreciation
I see the good in the world around me

Humility
I let my acts and accomplishments speak for themselves

Honesty
I am open and truthful

Judgement
I am open-minded and think carefully about my decisions

Empathy
I can put myself in other people's shoes

Teamwork
I like being part of a team and doing my part

Forgiveness
I believe that everyone deserves a second chance and do not hold grudges

MY PERSONAL STRENGTHS

My top three personal strengths are

1. _____

2. _____

3. _____

A time when I used my top three strengths was

1. _____

2. _____

3. _____

I demonstrate my top three strengths in my life and relationships by

1. _____

2. _____

3. _____

Others would say I am _____ because _____

_____

_____

A strength I would like to improve is _____. I could do this by _____

_____

_____

_____

Strengths I value in others are _____

_____

_____

A strength that has helped me achieve a goal is _____

_____

_____

A strength that makes me happy is _____ because _____

_____

_____

A challenge I have overcome by using my strengths is _____

_____

_____

INDIVIDUAL ACTIVITY

Identifying the Strengths in Others

Read the following two scenarios and answer the questions that follow.

COLM

Colm and his dads live in a terraced house on the outskirts of the city. Colm's parents have demanding jobs; one works very long hours. When Colm gets home from school, he empties the dishwasher and feeds their dog, Millie. After completing his homework, Colm takes Millie for a walk and makes sure that she has food in her bowl. When Colm's dad gets home from work and has done the weekly shop, Colm helps him to unpack the shopping and offers to make tea. They have a chat and prepare dinner together before his other dad arrives home. Colm shares any issues that arose throughout the day and loves hearing his dads' advice on any matters that troubled him, or even just anything funny that happened during the day. Colm goes to bed quite early and loves reading his favourite Marvel comics. In the morning, he goes for a jog before school as part of his football training.

- What personal strengths do you think Colm has?

  _____

  _____

- How does he demonstrate these strengths?

  _____

  _____

  _____

MICHELLE

Michelle lives with her parents in Cork City. Michelle loves playing basketball with the school team. She loves helping new members to learn the skills they need to improve. Michelle's mam has a debilitating illness, so Michelle is a carer for her on the days her dad is away on business. Michelle has had to miss some training sessions in order to help and support her mam. This does not bother her, as she loves helping her mam. She has spoken to her coach about the difficulties she is experiencing at home, and together they have agreed upon some training and skill development that she can do in her own time. Michelle is finding this very helpful, as it gives her some headspace and offers some time for escapism and self-care.

- What personal strengths do you think Michelle has?

  _____

  _____

  _____

- How does she demonstrate these strengths?

  _____

  _____

INDIVIDUAL ACTIVITY

Recognising the Strengths of Others

Think of a relationship you have with someone in your life – a friend, family member, coach, teacher or anyone else you are close to.

Name: _____   **Role in your life:** _____

What characteristics or strengths do you admire in this person? Why do you admire them?

_____

_____

_____

Praise and Giving Compliments

It is only from learning to know and appreciate ourselves that we can really begin to know and appreciate others. One way of making others feel good about themselves and recognising their strengths is by giving compliments.

CLASS DISCUSSION

1 Why is it important to acknowledge the strengths and qualities of others?

2 What praise or positive feedback have you received in the last week? Who gave you the compliment? What was said? How did you feel?

7 How can giving compliments foster a positive environment in school or among friends?

6 How can we accept a compliment?

3 How does it feel to get a genuine compliment? Why?

5 Why might it be difficult to accept a compliment?

4 How does giving compliments to others make us feel?

Use the prompts below to brainstorm what you could compliment others on.

Personal strengths • Qualities • Work ethic • Actions • Clothes

Tips for Giving Compliments

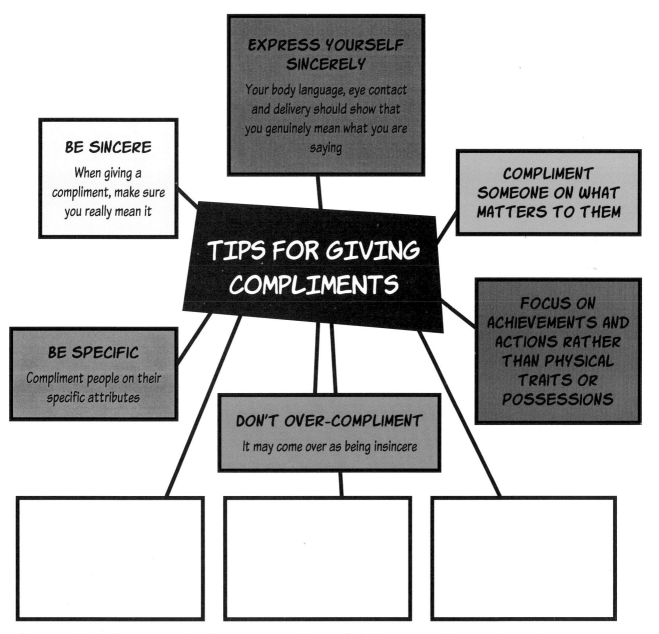

EXPRESS YOURSELF SINCERELY
Your body language, eye contact and delivery should show that you genuinely mean what you are saying

BE SINCERE
When giving a compliment, make sure you really mean it

COMPLIMENT SOMEONE ON WHAT MATTERS TO THEM

TIPS FOR GIVING COMPLIMENTS

FOCUS ON ACHIEVEMENTS AND ACTIONS RATHER THAN PHYSICAL TRAITS OR POSSESSIONS

BE SPECIFIC
Compliment people on their specific attributes

DON'T OVER-COMPLIMENT
It may come over as being insincere

Can you think of any other tips for giving compliments? Add your own ideas to the mind map.

Giving Compliments to Others in My Class

Write your name on the handle of the mirror below.

Look around the room and think of the personal strengths you admire in others. You are now going to move around the room and give your classmates compliments.

Walk around the classroom and swap your book with your classmates. When you receive someone else's book, write a compliment for them on their mirror. Swap your books back, then move on and find someone else. At the end of the session, you will have given lots of compliments **to** others and received lots of compliments **from** others.

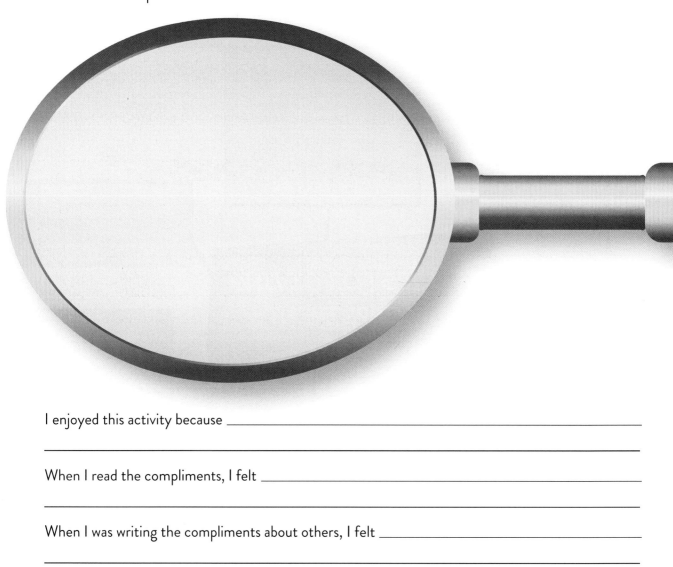

I enjoyed this activity because _____

_____

When I read the compliments, I felt _____

_____

When I was writing the compliments about others, I felt _____

_____

REFLECTION ON MY LEARNING

Speak to the person beside you and tell them what you think their strengths are.

LESSON 5

Who Am I?
Appreciating Difference

Learning Outcomes: 1.3, 1.4

 respected resilient aware connected responsible

By the end of this lesson, you will:

➡ recognise a range of factors that contribute to and influence your identity

➡ have reflected on what makes you who you are

➡ have discussed ways of celebrating diversity in our society

➡ have identified ways of making your school and community more inclusive.

KEYWORDS

Self-esteem
Self-image
Self-identity
Sexual orientation
Gender identity
Culture
Ethnic background

ADDITIONAL RESOURCES

www.BeLonG To.org BeLonG To is a national youth support service for gay, lesbian, bisexual and transgender young people. **Phone 01 670 6223.**

CLASS ACTIVITY

On a piece of paper, write **three** interesting facts about yourself. It can be something that people might not know or guess just by looking at you. Give your piece of paper to your teacher. The teacher will call out the facts and the rest of the class must guess who the person is.

Who am I?

What Makes Us Who We Are?

In the previous activity, we revealed something about ourselves. You saw that, although in many ways we are similar to our friends and classmates, we are all very different in our own unique way. We all have our unique identity that makes us who we are.

Self-identity:
What makes us who we are? Your self-identity is unique to you. Like your fingerprint, no two people have the same identity.

Write all the different things that could contribute to a person's identity around the figure below.

WHAT MAKES US WHO WE ARE?

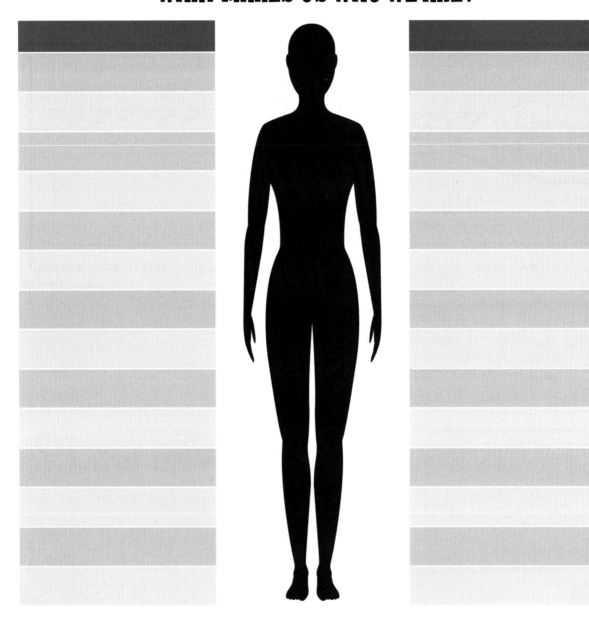

CLASS DISCUSSION

1 What are the different ways we express our identity to others? (For example, clothes, hairstyle)?

2 What does it mean to be 'true to yourself'?

9 How can we show respect for difference so people feel comfortable being their true selves?

3 How can being 'true to yourself' positively impact your life?

8 Do you think social media has an influence on how we portray ourselves or how others perceive us? In what way?

4 How can our friends and family influence our interests, how we behave and how we express ourselves?

7 Are there any rules at school that make it difficult for you to be your true self?

5 Are there any situations in which someone might hide their true self or identity? How might this feel?

6 Are there differences in the way different cultures express their identity?

Search YouTube for 'Wellbeing For Children: Identity And Values' (5:03) to learn more about identity and values.

INDIVIDUAL ACTIVITY

My True Self

The following guided visualisation will help you reflect on what makes you who you are and give you a deeper understanding of your own identity.

Take time to settle comfortably in your chair. Close your eyes, if you wish. Become aware of your breathing.

Imagine that you have left the classroom and you find yourself deep in the woods. You are going to walk deeper and deeper into the woods. You are surrounded by trees – you hear their branches shake in the wind. Birds are squawking in the sky. You can hear the flow and crash of a waterfall nearby.

As you walk on, you come to a clearing and notice a cottage. The front door is open. You're curious and go into the cottage. The cottage is dark and dusty. You walk inside and you find an old dusty chest that has your name on it. When you open it, you see that it is full of beautiful and memorable things that represent you, who you are and your life so far. Photographs of you with people in your life, family and friends and groups you are connected with and who have influenced you. Your culture. Good times you've had. Places with happy memories. Things you enjoy, like sport and hobbies. Your favourite clothes. The things you cherish, value and believe in. The things that are important to you in life. Your talents, and pictures of things that make you happy.

Become aware of how you feel when you see all these things. What are your strengths? What qualities do you bring to your family and friends? Are you considerate? Fun to be with? Helpful? Decide what memories and pictures you want to take from your treasure chest. Gently close the lid, and get ready to leave the cottage.

When you are ready, slowly and gently bring your awareness back to the classroom and open your eyes.

Source: Trust Manual Senior Cycle SPHE resource

INDIVIDUAL ACTIVITY

Use what you have taken from the treasure chest to complete your unique photo frame below.

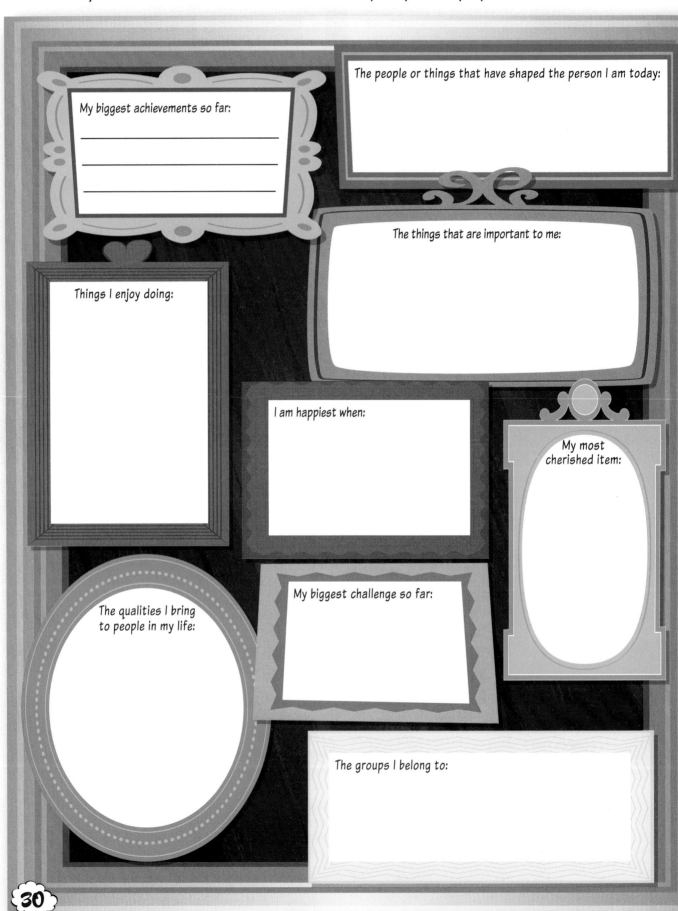

My biggest achievements so far:

The people or things that have shaped the person I am today:

The things that are important to me:

Things I enjoy doing:

I am happiest when:

My most cherished item:

The qualities I bring to people in my life:

My biggest challenge so far:

The groups I belong to:

CLASS DISCUSSION

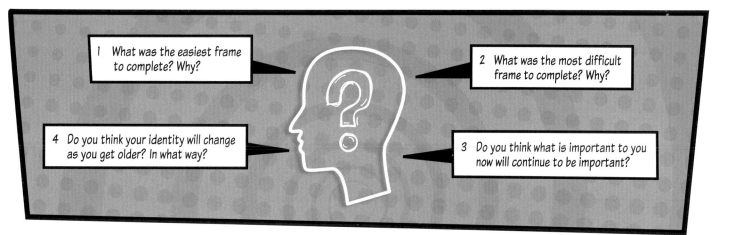

1. What was the easiest frame to complete? Why?

2. What was the most difficult frame to complete? Why?

4. Do you think your identity will change as you get older? In what way?

3. Do you think what is important to you now will continue to be important?

Respecting Difference and Diversity

It is important for us to recognise that we are all unique and we all have a special contribution to the world. Imagine a world where everyone was the same – it would be pretty boring.

Respecting difference means treating others with kindness, empathy and fairness regardless of their race, culture, beliefs, gender, sexual orientation or background. It helps to create a world where everyone feels valued and included.

KEYWORD

Inclusion means that diversity and difference is welcomed. Everyone is treated fairly and feels respected and valued in a group.

No one is better than anyone else

Accepting yourself for who you are

Treating others the way you would like to be treated

Believing that everyone should be treated with dignity and respect

Making others feel welcome

INCLUSION

Showing fairness towards others

Accepting others as they are

Not labelling or judging others

Accepting people with different beliefs or viewpoints to your own

Showing respect for difference

Inclusion Poem or Song

You are now going to create an acrostic poem, song or rap using the letters of the word 'inclusion'. Your poem or song doesn't have to rhyme, but it would be great if it did! Using each letter of 'inclusion' as the start of a line in your composition, create something that tells your teacher and classmates how to make your school more inclusive. For example, for the letter 'I', you could write 'Identifying ways we can make our school friendlier'.

I

N

C

L

U

S

I

O

N

REFLECTION ON MY LEARNING

I can be true to myself by:

_____

_____

_____

I can be respectful and inclusive to others in my school and community by:

_____

_____

LESSON 6

Goal Setting

Learning Outcome: 1.9

By the end of this lesson, you will:

•• understand the difference between vague and specific goals

•• understand the steps in goal setting

•• set personal goals for the year ahead.

KEYWORDS

Goal setting
Extrinsic motivation
Intrinsic motivation

ADDITIONAL RESOURCES

www.kidshealth.org Provides helpful information and practical advice on goal setting.

Goal Setting

If we want to achieve something in our lives, we have to create a plan and work towards making that plan happen. Goal setting helps to motivate us to achieve what we want.

CLASS DISCUSSION

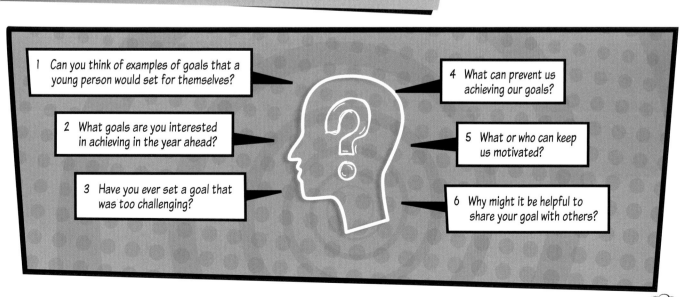

1. Can you think of examples of goals that a young person would set for themselves?

2. What goals are you interested in achieving in the year ahead?

3. Have you ever set a goal that was too challenging?

4. What can prevent us achieving our goals?

5. What or who can keep us motivated?

6. Why might it be helpful to share your goal with others?

INDIVIDUAL ACTIVITY

Letter from My Future Self

Have you thought about what you want to achieve this year?
You are now going to write yourself a letter from summer
this year. Imagine that you have achieved all that you had
hoped to achieve.

These can be achievements in your personal life, your
school life, your school subjects, sports, hobbies or with
your friends and family.

In the letter to yourself, you are telling yourself about
the school year, what you set out to achieve and what
you achieved.

You can mention some obstacles you encountered, if
there were any.

Dear _____   Date _____

_____

_____

_____

_____

_____

_____

_____

_____

_____

_____

_____

_____

_____

_____

_____

_____

_____

_____

Achieving My Goals

Now that you have thought about what you want to achieve this year, it is important to set goals. A goal broken down into steps becomes **a plan**.

INDIVIDUAL ACTIVITY

Make Your Goals Specific

When you set a goal, you should make sure they are very clear about what you want to achieve. For example, 'I want to get fit' is very vague and hard to achieve. A more specific goal is 'I want to run 5km in 25 minutes' – this is much easier to achieve.

How would you make the following goals more specific?

1. Get better at playing guitar
2. Save money
3. Eat more healthily
4. Read more books
5. Improve my grade in Maths

1. _____

2. _____

3. _____

4. _____

5. _____

Motivation

Think about why you want to achieve your goal. Is it intrinsic or extrinsic?

Intrinsic motivation comes from **within** the person. You choose to do the activity because it is internally rewarding, you choose to do it because it is fun or rewarding, or it makes you feel good.

Extrinsic motivation comes from **outside** the person. You are motivated to achieve the goal from external rewards in return. Examples of extrinsic motivation include rewards such as trophies, praise from others and money.

Steps

To achieve your goal, you need to break it down into a few steps. In this example, you want to improve your grade in Maths. You can break that goal down into five steps:

Step 1: Decide how much extra time you want to spend studying Maths.

Step 2: Get a parent/guardian/tutor on board to help you.

Step 3: Look at your Maths course and decide what you need to work on.

Step 4: Create a study plan.

Step 5: Revise and practise answering exam questions.

Obstacles

What do you think might get in the way of you achieving your goal?

In the example of improving your grade in Maths, you might see less of your friends if you spend more time studying.

Date

Identifying a timeframe for achieving your goal is very important.

Giving yourself a deadline is a great motivation. In the Maths example, your deadline could be the Maths mock exam. Giving yourself deadlines or goal dates also helps you to keep track of your progress.

In the diagram below, fill in your goal for this term, your motivation for achieving your goal, the steps you will take, the obstacles you may encounter along the way, and the date you hope to achieve your goal.

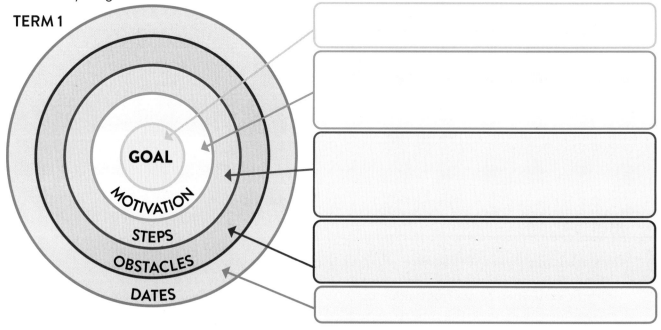

TERM 1

GOAL

MOTIVATION

STEPS

OBSTACLES

DATES

INDIVIDUAL ACTIVITY

You have completed your goal plan for Term 1. Throughout the year, go back and set your goals for each term on the next page.

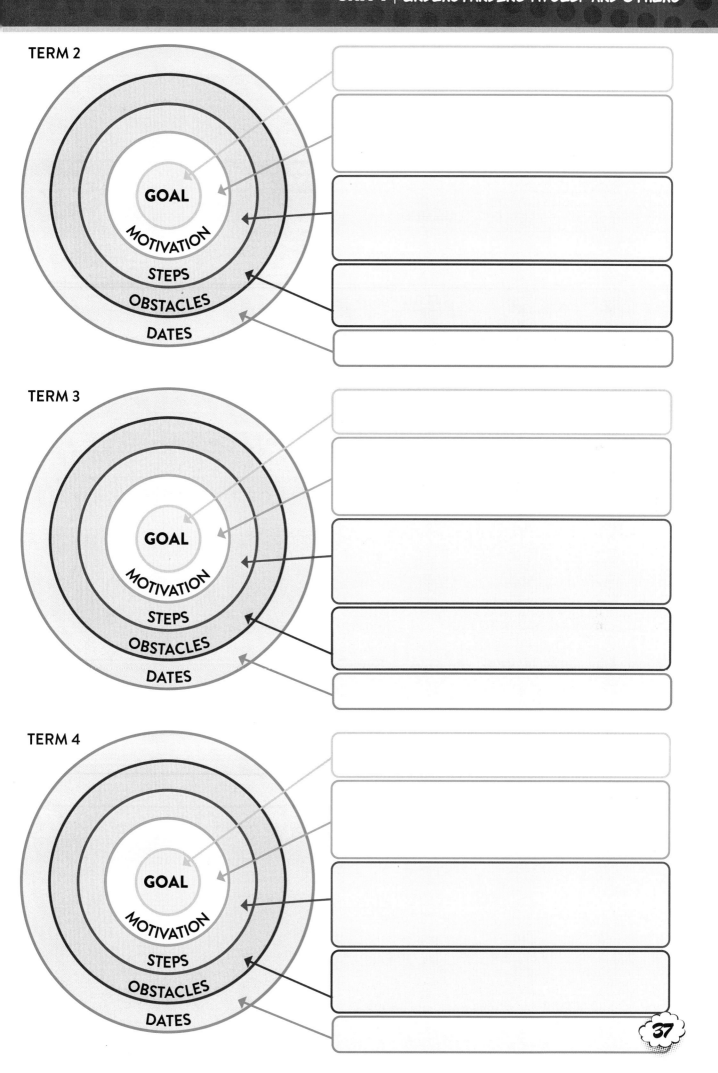

TERM 2

GOAL

MOTIVATION

STEPS

OBSTACLES

DATES

TERM 3

GOAL

MOTIVATION

STEPS

OBSTACLES

DATES

TERM 4

GOAL

MOTIVATION

STEPS

OBSTACLES

DATES

LESSON 7
Understanding Empathy

Learning Outcomes: 1.7, 1.8, 4.2

resilient   respected   responsible   connected

By the end of this lesson, you will:

- be able to explain what empathy means
- understand the difference between empathy and sympathy
- reflect on how you can support other people in challenging times.

KEYWORDS

Empathy
Sympathy

ADDITIONAL RESOURCES

Text 50808 A free, anonymous 24-hour messaging service that provides everything from a calming chat to immediate support. This text service is a safe space where you are listened to by a trained volunteer. By asking questions, listening to you and responding with support, they will help you sort through your feelings until you both feel you are in a calm, safe place.

www.ispcc.ie/teenline A national 24-hour helpline service for teenagers up to the age of 18 in Ireland. They can be contacted 24 hours a day, 365 days a year, online or by calling **1800 833 634**.

GROUP ACTIVITY

Go to YouTube and search for 'Inside Out Sadness comforts Bing Bong' (2:36) to watch a video from a children's movie.

What are the different approaches that Joy and Sadness use to comfort Bing Bong?

_____

_____

_____

_____

How does Sadness manage to make him feel better?

_____

_____

_____

_____

What Is Empathy?

If someone told you that they hit their funny bone on a piece of furniture, or stood on a piece of Lego in their bare feet, you would immediately know what that felt like. If someone shared a difficult experience with you that you had been through yourself, you would have no problem understanding how they are feeling. This is called empathy.

In the previous lesson, we learned about the benefits of recognising and expressing our feelings to our overall health and wellbeing. In this lesson, we will explore how to acknowledge the feelings of others and how best to support them.

The Difference between Empathy and Sympathy

Sympathy	Empathy
What is sympathy? Sympathy is about feeling pity, sorrow or concern for someone else. You feel sorry for what someone else is going through, but you can't share how they are feeling.	**What is empathy?** Empathy is the ability to understand what other people are thinking or feeling; you see things from their point of view. Empathy is sometimes described as being able to 'put yourself in someone else's shoes'. If we see someone unhappy or going through a difficult time, we can share what they are feeling and support them.
Real-life example You are aware that a classmate is upset because an embarrassing picture of them is circulating online.	
A sympathetic response would be feeling sorry for your classmate.	An empathetic response would be understanding how you would feel or react if the same picture was posted of you, asking people to stop sharing the photo, and letting your classmate know you understand what they are going through.

 Go to YouTube and search for 'Brené Brown on Empathy vs Sympathy' (2:53) to learn more about the difference between empathy and sympathy.

39

INDIVIDUAL ACTIVITY

It Is How We Say It

Below are different statements from people showing empathy and sympathy. Put an 'E' beside the statements you think show empathy and an 'S' beside the statements you think show sympathy.

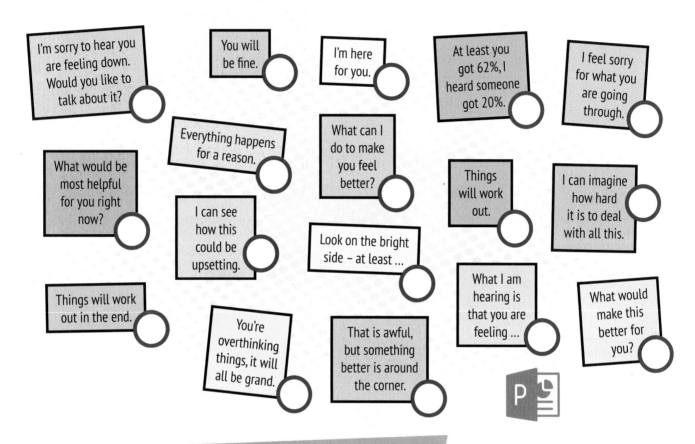

I'm sorry to hear you are feeling down. Would you like to talk about it? ○

You will be fine. ○

I'm here for you. ○

At least you got 62%, I heard someone got 20%. ○

I feel sorry for what you are going through. ○

Everything happens for a reason. ○

What can I do to make you feel better? ○

Things will work out. ○

I can imagine how hard it is to deal with all this. ○

What would be most helpful for you right now? ○

I can see how this could be upsetting. ○

Look on the bright side – at least ... ○

Things will work out in the end. ○

You're overthinking things, it will all be grand. ○

That is awful, but something better is around the corner. ○

What I am hearing is that you are feeling ... ○

What would make this better for you? ○

CLASS DISCUSSION

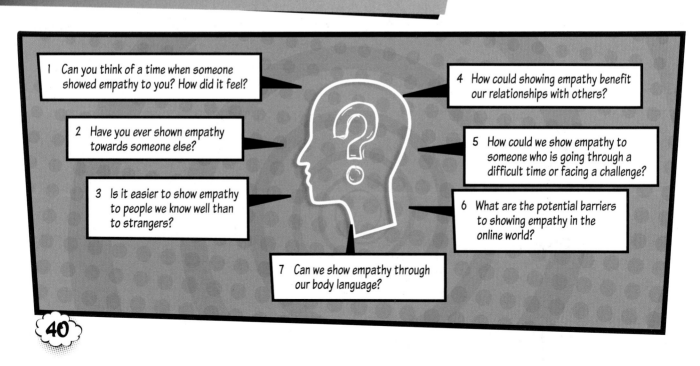

1 Can you think of a time when someone showed empathy to you? How did it feel?

2 Have you ever shown empathy towards someone else?

3 Is it easier to show empathy to people we know well than to strangers?

4 How could showing empathy benefit our relationships with others?

5 How could we show empathy to someone who is going through a difficult time or facing a challenge?

6 What are the potential barriers to showing empathy in the online world?

7 Can we show empathy through our body language?

INDIVIDUAL ACTIVITY

Empathy vs Sympathy Quiz

1. **Which of the following statements is true about empathy?**

    A. Empathy is about 'putting yourself in someone else's shoes'. ☐

    B. Empathy allows you to see things from the other person's point of view. ☐

    C. Empathy is thinking about how you would feel if you were in a similar situation. ☐

    D. All of the above. ☐

2. **Which of the following statements is true about sympathy?**

    A. Sympathy is feeling sorry for what someone else is going through, but not understanding how they are feeling. ☐

    B. Sympathy is looking at the situation from the other person's viewpoint. ☐

    C. Sympathy is about 'putting yourself in someone else's shoes'. ☐

    D. All of the above. ☐

3. **Does this scenario show empathy or sympathy?**

    Ellie is in third year. Her brother is in sixth class but is nervous about his first week in secondary school. Ellie goes for a walk with him and asks him how he is feeling and what his main concerns are. She reassures him that she understands how nervous he is feeling and that she is always there if he wants to talk to her about anything.

    Empathy ☐   Sympathy ☐

4. **Does this scenario show empathy or sympathy?**

    Barry texts Ali to tell her he had a crush on her. Ali showed the text to others in her friend group, and some of them teased Barry online about this. Barry tells his friend Ger what has happened. Ger says, 'It's embarrassing, but you'll be fine. It will be forgotten about in no time.'

    Empathy ☐   Sympathy ☐

5. **Does this scenario show empathy or sympathy?**

    Bob's dog Buddy died. Bob has had Buddy since he was a baby, so he is very upset and he is finding it difficult to concentrate in class. Lauren, who sits next to him in Maths class, sees that he is not himself and asks him if he is OK. When he tells her what happened, Lauren says, 'I can imagine what you are going through, because I have a dog too. You must really miss him.'

    Empathy ☐   Sympathy ☐

6. **Does this scenario show empathy or sympathy?**

    Simon's sister Zuzanna is very upset, as she has broken up with her boyfriend. He knows she really liked him, but Simon wasn't too fond of him. Simon says, 'Don't worry about it, you were too good for him. There are plenty more fish in the sea!'

    Empathy ☐   Sympathy ☐

41

7. Does this scenario show empathy or sympathy?

Amy's parents are arguing a lot, and she is afraid they might break up. This is upsetting Amy so much that it is affecting her schoolwork. She confides in her friend Lucy about what is happening at home. Lucy says, 'If there is anything I can do to help, just ask. I am always here to talk and listen.'

Empathy ☐   Sympathy ☐

8. Does this picture show empathy or sympathy?

I know how you feel

Empathy ☐   Sympathy ☐

9. Which side of the picture shows empathy?

I've been there.

I feel so bad for you.

Left ☐
Right ☐

10. Which side of the picture shows empathy?

I feel sad to know you are suffering.

I'm here and I understand your suffering.

Left ☐
Right ☐

11. You can show empathy by:

A. Not judging others ☐

B. Using encouraging body language, like nodding ☐

C. Listening ☐

D. All of the above ☐

You may not be able to feel empathy in some situations. That's OK – everyone's experiences are unique, so you won't always be able to understand exactly what they are going through. Try your best to help and support the person anyway.

INDIVIDUAL ACTIVITY

Walk in My Shoes

Imagine you are the person in one of the photographs below. Write a story for the person, from their perspective, explaining the story behind the photograph. In your story, try to put yourself in the person's shoes and describe how the person is thinking, feeling and behaving.

CLASS DISCUSSION

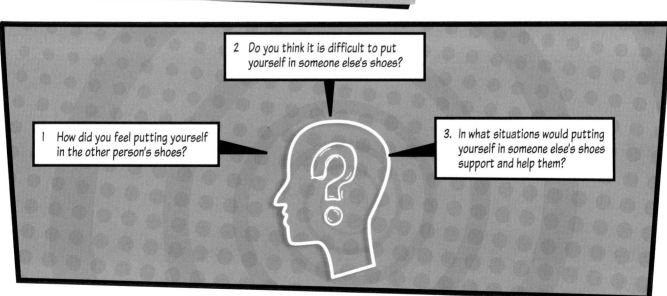

2 Do you think it is difficult to put yourself in someone else's shoes?

1 How did you feel putting yourself in the other person's shoes?

3. In what situations would putting yourself in someone else's shoes support and help them?

Below are some challenging situations a young person may find themselves in. Your teacher will assign you one scenario. Discuss the scenario and then answer the questions in the placemat below.

Someone whose parents are constantly arguing

Someone whose dog has just died

Someone who has just moved from another country and has little English

Someone who shared a nude picture and is now being blackmailed

Someone whose classmates created a fake profile of them on social media

Someone who has lost the county final and they gave away a penalty

Someone who has just joined your class and is looking nervous

Someone who let slip a secret about a close friend and has fallen out with them

Someone who is being teased and excluded by a group of students

Someone who thinks they might be gay

Someone who sits alone during lunchtime every day

Someone who has fallen out with their friend group

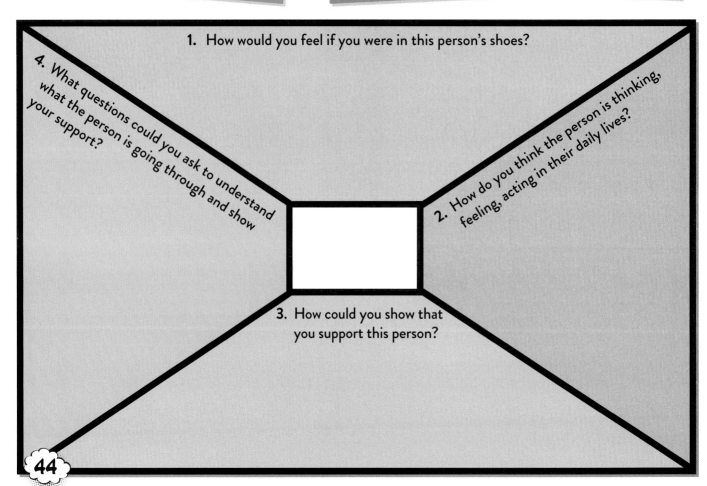

1. How would you feel if you were in this person's shoes?

4. What questions could you ask to understand what the person is going through and show your support?

2. How do you think the person is thinking, feeling, acting in their daily lives?

3. How could you show that you support this person?

REFLECTION ON MY LEARNING

A way I could show empathy and support to someone is

_____

_____

_____

> Your group has been tasked with organising a 'Respect for All' day in your school. The purpose of the day is to raise awareness about the importance of everyone feeling respected and included in the school community. Create a poster on an A3 page to promote the day.
>
> Your poster should include:
>
> ◯ A title
> ◯ The purpose of the day
> ◯ A schedule of activities that will be taking place
> ◯ The times, locations and classes involved

ANTI-BULLYING

LESSON 8

Friendship

Learning Outcomes: 3.1, 4.4

responsible   connected   respected

By the end of this lesson, you will:

↪ identify what makes a healthy or unhealthy friendship

↪ understand the qualities and skills that help make and maintain friendships

↪ recognise the qualities that you bring to your friendships.

KEYWORDS

Qualities
Healthy friendships
Unhealthy friendships

ADDITIONAL RESOURCES

www.reachout.com Information and support on maintaining and ending friendships.

www.cyh.com Go to the 'Friends' section for useful tips on making and keeping friends.

www.kidshealth.org Search 'good friends' for information on friendship and relationships.

What Do You Value in Friendships?

GROUP ACTIVITY

As we go through our teenage years, our friendships become very important in our lives. Having close, supportive friends can improve our overall wellbeing and help us deal with any challenges that life may throw at us. These close friendships also help nurture qualities such as empathy, loyalty, honesty, respect, compromise, understanding and acceptance.

It is important to recognise the qualities and behaviours you value in friendships. Scattered around the Diamond 9 below are different qualities and behaviours that young people value in friendships. In a small group, use the Diamond 9 to rank how important you think these qualities are.

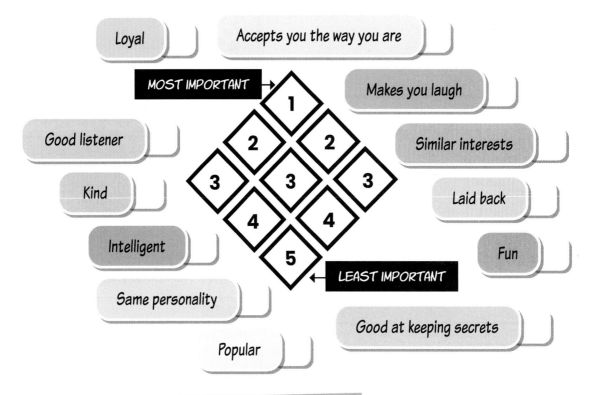

Loyal · Accepts you the way you are · Good listener · Kind · Intelligent · Same personality · Popular · Makes you laugh · Similar interests · Laid back · Fun · Good at keeping secrets

MOST IMPORTANT → 1, 2, 2, 3, 3, 3, 4, 4, 5 ← LEAST IMPORTANT

CLASS DISCUSSION

1 What made your group decide on the least important quality?

2 What qualities of friendship do you think are important in an online setting? Is an online friendship different from an in-person friendship?

3 How do you think social media influences our friendships?

4 How could you recognise that an online friendship was unhealthy?

5 Does the number of friends we have online or offline matter? Why?

Healthy and Unhealthy Friendships

Our friendships can change throughout our lives. There are friendships that stand the test of time, and there are those that drift apart, for any one of a number of reasons. Recognising what makes friendships healthy or unhealthy can help us to protect and maintain friendships that have a positive impact on us and let go of relationships that don't add anything to our lives.

INDIVIDUAL ACTIVITY

Red Flag, Green Flag

Below are characteristics of healthy and unhealthy behaviours in friendships. If you think it is a healthy characteristic, tick the green flag. If you think it is an unhealthy characteristic, tick the red flag. If you are unsure, do not tick either flag.

1.	Your friend sometimes embarrasses you in front of others.		
2.	You are your true self with your friend; you can share your opinions and feelings honestly.		
3.	If you tell your friend something personal, you are worried that they will tell other people.		
4.	Your friend is happy when good things happen for you.		
5.	Your friend posts pictures of you online without your permission.		
6.	Your friend always has your back, is loyal to you and supports you.		
7.	Your friend has not invited you to events even though other friends were invited.		
8.	You say you agree with your friend even though you don't, as you are afraid that they won't be your friend any more if you disagree with them.		
9.	If you and your friend have a disagreement, you talk about it and still stay friends.		
10.	You enjoy the time you spend with this friend but also enjoy spending time with other friends.		
11.	Your friend pressures you into doing things you don't want to do.		
12.	Your friend is jealous of your friendships with others.		
13.	Your friend sometimes does not reply to your text messages.		
14.	Your friend always agrees with what you say.		

CLASS DISCUSSION

1. Was it difficult to agree on what was a red flag and what was a green flag in a friendship?

2. For the red-flag statements, why do you think this would be a cause for concern in a friendship? What could someone do to deal with this situation or improve the friendship?

3. For the statements you were unsure about, why were you unsure?

4. Is there any situation where you think you should end a friendship?

5. How could you end a friendship respectfully?

- If there are arguments or disagreements, sit down and listen to each other's side of things.

- Be yourself. Don't pretend to be someone you're not – this never works, and people see through it.

- Don't pressure your friends into doing things they are not comfortable with. Accept their decisions.

- Be open, and don't be afraid to share your opinions and feelings.

- Treat your friends the way you would like to be treated.

- Accept your friends for who they are and don't try to change them.

- Don't talk about your friends behind their backs.

- Be kind. Do nice things for your friends.

- Have empathy. This means putting yourself in your friends' shoes to understand where they are coming from.

- Listen to others; don't just talk about yourself all the time.

GROUP ACTIVITY

Friendship Dilemmas

Scenario 1

Sal, Pamela and Nora always hang out together and have been friends since primary school. Sal and Pamela had a disagreement and are not talking now, but they both expect Nora to take their side.

1. What is the issue in this friendship?

_____

_____

2. Can the issue be resolved, and can the friendship be saved? Why?

_____

_____

3. What should Nora do next?

_____

_____

Scenario 2

Kerry and Ella are best friends. Kerry has a new boyfriend. She now spends very little time with Ella. Sometimes, Kerry does not reply to Ella's texts. Ella is worried about their friendship.

1. What is the issue in this friendship?

_____

_____

2. Can the issue be resolved, and can the friendship be saved? Why?

_____

_____

3. What should Ella do next?

_____

_____

Go to next page ...

Scenario 3

Yvette and Trish have been friends for a long time. Whenever they are with their larger group of friends, Yvette keeps trying to humiliate Trish by bringing up embarrassing things Trish did when they were younger. When they are alone, Trish asks Yvette not to do this, as it makes her feel bad, but Yvette continues to ridicule Trish when the others are around.

1. What is the issue in this friendship?

_____

_____

2. Can the issue be resolved, and can the friendship be saved? Why?

_____

_____

3. What should Trish do next?

_____

_____

Scenario 4

Alex and Sam have been best friends since primary school. On entering secondary school, they were placed in different classes. Alex has made good friends with girls and boys in her new class. Alex is spending more time now with her new friends and, more often than not, she doesn't invite Sam to join them. Sam has seen pictures of Alex out having fun with her new classmates and this upsets him.

1. What is the issue in this friendship?

_____

_____

2. Can the issue be resolved, and can the friendship be saved? Why?

_____

_____

3. What should Sam do next?

_____

_____

Scenario 5

Derek and Sam had an argument before the summer holidays. They haven't spoken since. When they returned to school after the summer break, their SPHE teacher paired them to work together on their CBA. They both find this situation very awkward.

1. What is the issue in this friendship?

_____

_____

2. Can the issue be resolved, and can the friendship be saved? Why?

_____

_____

3. What should Derek and Sam do next?

_____

_____

Scenario 6

Clem and Jamie are great friends. Recently, Clem told Jamie that he is feeling quite down because his parents are breaking up. Clem asked Jamie to promise not to tell anybody. After training, when they are packing up to go home, another teammate sits beside Clem and says, 'Jamie told me about your parents. I hope you are doing OK.'

1. What is the issue in this friendship?

_____

_____

2. Can the issue be resolved, and can the friendship be saved? Why?

_____

_____

3. What should Clem do next?

_____

_____

INDIVIDUAL ACTIVITY

Letter to a Good Friend

Write a letter to thank someone you believe is a good friend to you.
Remember: a friend can be a cousin, a neighbour, a brother or a sister!

In your letter, include:

1. The qualities the person you have chosen has as a friend
2. What you value about this friendship
3. How the friendship makes you feel
4. Funny memories you share
5. The positive impact your friend has had on your life.

Dear _____   Date _____

_____

_____

_____

_____

_____

_____

_____

_____

_____

_____

_____

_____

_____

_____

_____

_____

REFLECTION ON MY LEARNING

Think about what you want and don't want in a friendship by completing the following activity.

A friend to me is someone who ...	What I don't want in a friendship is ...
What I want to feel like in a friendship is ...	What I do not want to do or feel like in a friendship is ...
Qualities I bring to my friendships are ...	

LESSON 9 — Dealing with Bullying

Learning Outcomes: 4.4, 4.6, 4.7

responsible   connected   respected

By the end of this lesson, you will:

- recognise different types of abusive and bullying behaviour online and in person
- describe the impact of bullying behaviour on a person
- identify how to deal with incidences of abusive and bullying behaviour.

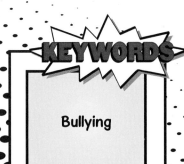

KEYWORDS

Bullying

ADDITIONAL RESOURCES

www.tacklebullying.ie A national website to help young people, parents and teachers counter bullying and cyberbullying.

www.webwise.ie Webwise is an Irish internet safety awareness centre. This website has a youth section which provides tips and advice on bullying and cyberbullying.

www.barnardos.ie Provides information and advice on how to deal with bullying.

Text 50808 A free, anonymous 24-hour messaging service that provides everything from a calming chat to immediate support. This text service is a safe space where you are listened to by a trained volunteer. By asking questions, listening to you and responding with support, they will help you sort through your feelings until you both feel you are now in a calm, safe place.

Effects of Bullying

Bullying is when, through their words or actions, someone repeatedly causes harm or distress to another person. Bullying is about someone having power or control over another person, leaving the bullied person lacking confidence, feeling frightened and isolated. Being bullied can seriously affect a person's health, wellbeing and school life. Someone who is being bullied may be afraid to speak out because of embarrassment or fear of what might happen to them if they do.

No one has the right to bully another person – we should always treat others with the same dignity and respect we would like others to treat us with. We should be conscious of how our words and our actions can hurt others, even if sometimes we don't mean them to.

Bullying has a negative impact on everyone involved, so whether you are the victim of bullying, have witnessed bullying or think you might be bullying someone else, asking for help or speaking out is so important.

In this lesson, we will look at the different types of bullying and different ways of dealing with bullying when it occurs.

INDIVIDUAL ACTIVITY

Bullying 4321

 4 words I think of when I hear the word bullying

_____

_____

_____

_____

 3 feelings I associate with bullying

_____

_____

_____

 2 people or supports that could help if I was being bullied

_____

_____

 1 word that would describe how a victim of bullying might feel if they got support

_____

INDIVIDUAL ACTIVITY

There are many different types of bullying. Match the type of bullying to the correct description by writing the letter of the type of bullying beside its description.

Description	
1. Involves saying nasty things to hurt other people's feelings, e.g. about their sexuality, appearance, clothes, ethnicity, family.	
2. Threatening to hurt a person to force them to hand over money or to do something they don't want to do. Can often happen online.	
3. Often takes place in friend groups and involves trying to make someone feel bad by, e.g., eye-rolling, whispering, passing notes, mimicking, laughing behind someone's back with other group members. Less easy to pinpoint than physical bullying and can go unnoticed for a long time. Difficult to describe and report, especially because the person acting this way can often seem friendly in other situations.	
4. Involves actions such as: kicking, tripping, hair-pulling, punching, spitting, poking, fighting, etc. It can also involve damaging a person's property, e.g. books, clothes.	
5. Involves threatening body language and non-verbal signs to intimidate another person.	
6. Targeted at a person because of their actual or perceived identity group, such as: sexual orientation, gender identity, disability, ethnicity, religion, immigration status, etc.	
7. Using information technology and social media to bully someone online. Takes the form of threatening or hurtful messages by email, text, or posting on social media sites.	
8. Where a person is deliberately ignored and/or left out of conversations, activities and online groups to make them feel isolated.	

Type of bullying		
	A. Physical bullying	**E.** Relational bullying
	B. Exclusion bullying	**F.** Verbal bullying
	C. Cyberbullying	**G.** Identity-based bullying
	D. Gesture bullying	**H.** Extortion bullying

INDIVIDUAL ACTIVITY

Read the following scenarios and answer the questions that follow each one.

The Football Game

Danny is in 1st Year in school. He is very outspoken and often talks out of turn in class. Danny doesn't mean to be cheeky, but he is very interested in lots of different subjects and likes to discuss things with his teachers. Lately, Danny has noticed that some of the other students start laughing when he talks. In particular, two boys from his primary school, Conor and Jack, make fun of Danny whenever he says anything.

Danny is quite good at soccer, and he plays with the school team. One day after losing a match, Danny and the rest of the team are getting changed in the changing rooms. Conor and Jack are on the team too, and they are not happy about losing. They blame Danny for losing the match, saying that he did not mark his man properly. Danny tries to ignore them and continues getting changed. Then Conor shouts that they will never win anything with a gay person on the team. He goes over to Danny and pushes him. Danny falls backwards and lands on the floor, and Conor starts kicking him. Everyone else in the dressing room starts to shout, 'Fight, fight, fight!' and some of the team take out their phones to record it.

Eventually the coach comes in and stops the fight. He tries to find out what happened, but no one is willing to tell him. The school is holding an investigation into what happened. Meanwhile, Danny can't face his team, or face going to school.

1. What type/s of bullying is Danny experiencing?

_____

_____

2. Describe how Danny must have felt after he was beaten up in the changing room and the event was recorded. Describe as many emotions as you can.

_____

_____

_____

_____

3. Do you think this type of bullying is typical among boys or girls?

_____

_____

_____

4. Is there anyone who could have helped Danny? How could they have helped?

_____

_____

_____

_____

The New School

Jemma's family moved house, so she has to start at a new secondary school. She was nervous at first, because she didn't know anyone at her new school. However, she has settled in and made friends quickly with a group of girls. Nicole is the ringleader of the group, and the other girls look up to her. Nicole often says mean things about other girls in their year group, which Jemma doesn't like, but Jemma really likes the other girls in the group. She has started to meet up with them at the weekends, going shopping and hanging out at the park or at each other's houses. They have also started hanging out and meeting up with a group of boys from the other school at the weekends. Jemma really fancies James, a boy from the group, and he seems to like her too. Last weekend, Jemma ended up talking to James for a long time at the disco.

When Jemma comes to school on Monday morning, the girls are really horrible to her – talking under their hands, raising their eyes and sniggering at her when she passes. When she finishes school, Jemma turns on her phone to find a number of nasty text messages from the girls. One of them says, 'You knew Nicole liked James, how could you do that?'

As the week goes on, Jemma is excluded from the WhatsApp group, and she is receiving mean messages at all hours of the day. Jemma is trying to ignore them, but it is really upsetting her at school and she feels constantly worried about what they will do. They have started bumping into her in the corridors and laughing while calling her names. They have also written nasty things about her on the back of the toilet door. Jemma is now afraid to go to school.

1. What types of bullying is Jemma experiencing?

_____

_____

2. How do you think Jemma is being affected by the bullying?

_____

_____

_____

_____

3. What could happen to improve this situation for Jemma?

_____

_____

_____

4. Who could play a role in sorting out this bullying issue?

_____

_____

_____

_____

Tips for dealing with bullying

Try speaking to the bully. If you feel safe and comfortable doing so, try to speak to the bully about how their behaviour is making you feel. You may ask them why they are doing this to you. When telling the bully how their behaviour is affecting you, use 'I' statements, e.g. 'I feel ... when you ...' Try to make sure that other people are around when you confront the bully. If confronting the bully is too difficult, then don't.

Use positive self-talk. Tell yourself that you do not deserve to be treated this way and that what the bully is saying is not true.

Ignore it. Try to ignore the behaviour and try not to show that you are upset. This is hard, but bullies thrive on other people's reactions and/or fears. If they don't get a reaction, they may give up.

Walk away from the situation. Try to walk away from the situation. Try not to fight back or use violence. This can only make things worse.

Use humour. Try to use humour to lighten the mood if the situation allows.

Get support from your friends. Try to make sure that you do not become isolated in the presence of the bully. Try to get support from your friends. If your group of friends are responsible for the bullying, you need to consider leaving that friend group and making new friends.

Tell a trusted adult. If you find that you cannot turn to friends or deal with the bullying yourself, you need to tell a trusted adult. If the bullying is serious, it needs to be reported to the school.

Could You Be a Bully?

These questions will help you to reflect on your own behaviour.

(a) Have you ever hurt someone on purpose?

(b) Have you ever deliberately tried to make someone else feel bad by saying something hurtful or knowingly excluding them from a situation?

(c) Have you ever picked on someone younger than you?

(d) Do you spread rumours knowing that they are not true?

(e) Have you tried to turn your friends against someone?

(f) Have you ever laughed along with a bully?

(g) Have you ever used the excuse that you were only messing when you know that you were not?

If answering these questions has made you feel uneasy, then you need to think about how you treat others. If you are bullying someone, you can stop by doing the following:

- Apologise to the person face to face or write them an apology letter.
- Repair the damage done by removing insulting pictures or harmful messages.
- Talk to a parent or teacher about what you have done and seek advice on how to rectify the situation.

Why do you behave this way?

- Why do you feel the need to pick on other people?
- Have you been or are you being bullied, and are you angry about this?
- Do you make someone else feel small to make yourself feel better?
- Is there something you enjoy about making someone else feel bad? If so, why? Is it fair?
- Do you think your behaviour makes you look and feel powerful?

If you answer yes to any of these statements, then you need to face up to what you are doing and talk to a trusted adult for advice.

GROUP ACTIVITY

Anti-Bullying Poem/Rap

You are now going to create an acrostic poem, song or rap using the letters of the phrase 'Anti-Bullying'. Your poem or song doesn't have to rhyme, but it would be great if it did! Use each letter of 'Anti-Bullying' as the start of a line in your composition. For example, for the letter 'A', you could write 'All people deserve kindness and respect'. When you have completed your poem or rap, decorate it on a large poster sheet and display it on your classroom wall or around the school.

A
N
T
I
B
U
L
L
Y
I
N
G

REFLECTION ON MY LEARNING

Three things I have learned about bullying in this lesson are:

As a result of this lesson, I will:

1. _____
2. _____
3. _____

_____
_____
_____

Bullying is Everyone's Business

Learning Outcomes: 4.4, 4.8

connected   responsible   resilient

By the end of this lesson, you will:

- ➥ understand the role of bystander and upstander in bullying
- ➥ explain the importance of standing up to or reporting bullying or abusive behaviour
- ➥ identify what you can do if you witness abusive or bullying behaviour
- ➥ explore the reason why people might be reluctant to stand up to bullying.

KEYWORDS

Upstander
Bystander

ADDITIONAL RESOURCES

www.tacklebullying.ie A national website to help young people, parents and teachers counter bullying and cyberbullying.

www.webwise.ie Webwise is an Irish internet safety awareness centre. This website has a youth section which provides tips and advice on bullying and cyberbullying.

www.barnardos.ie Provides information and advice on how to deal with bullying.

Bystanders and Bullying

In the previous lesson, you explored how bullying can negatively impact a person's health and wellbeing. The key message is that bullying is never OK. It creates an environment of fear and can negatively impact everyone involved.

Witnessing bullying can be extremely distressing and uncomfortable. People are sometimes afraid to speak out, as they fear being labelled a snitch or becoming a target themselves. Knowing the damaging effects of bullying, everyone has a key role in speaking out and stopping it. In this lesson, we will explore the role of the bystander and upstander in incidences of bullying.

INDIVIDUAL ACTIVITY

The following activity will help you reflect on your opinions on bullying or abusive behaviour. Read the following statements and place the letter corresponding to the statement on the scale. The left end of the scale means you strongly disagree with the statement and the right end means you strongly agree with the statement.

STRONGLY DISAGREE   STRONGLY AGREE

A. It is up to parents and teachers to sort out bullying issues.

B. I would know how to get support if I was bullied or a witness to a bullying incident.

C. Cyberbullying is worse than real-life bullying.

D. Bullying is not always obvious to others; it can be very subtle and difficult to explain.

E. Boys and girls bully in different ways.

F. It is sometimes difficult to intervene if you witness bullying.

G. Students have a role to play in the prevention of bullying.

H. Our school is a safe place, free from bullying.

I. If I tell a parent or teacher about bullying, it will just get worse.

J. If I am aware that someone is being bullied, I should stand up for them.

Upstanders and Bystanders

An **upstander** is someone who recognises when something is wrong and acts to make it right. When an upstander sees or hears about someone being bullied, they speak up and do their best to help, protect and support the person.

A **bystander** is someone who knows about or sees bullying happening to someone else. They do not take part in the bullying but do nothing to prevent or stop it.

The Four Types of Bystander

Assistants: They do not start the bullying but take an active part by joining in and supporting the bully.

Reinforcers: They do not take an active part, but their words or actions encourage the bully, e.g. laughing along, adding comments online, making the situation worse.

Outsiders: They watch or know what is happening but don't speak out or try to stop the bullying. They may take the view it is none of their business or they could dislike the bullying but are unsure what to do or are afraid to intervene.

Defenders: Upstanders. They support the person being bullied. When they see or hear about someone being bullied, they speak up and do their best to help, protect and support the person.

The Bystander Effect

 Go to YouTube and search for 'The Bystander Effect Science of Empathy' (5.36). After watching the video, discuss the questions below with your classmates.

CLASS DISCUSSION

3 How can bystanders play a role in stopping bullying without putting themselves in danger?

1 How do you think the bystander effect relates to bullying in real life and online?

2 What might prevent someone intervening or taking action to stop bullying?

4 How do you think standing up to bullying can help the bully as well as the person being bullied?

5 What can someone do if they witness or know of someone being bullied?

The ABCs of Being an Upstander

Before intervening in a bullying situation, try the ABC approach.

Assess the situation for safety: If you see someone being bullied, ask yourself if you can help safely. Remember, your personal safety is a priority – never put yourself at risk.

Be in a group: It's safer to call out bullying behaviour or intervene in a group. If this is not an option, report it to others, for example a teacher, parent or other responsible adult who can act.

Care for the victim: Talk to the person who you think may need help. Ask them if they are OK, tell them that you don't agree with what is happening and that you are there to support them.

INDIVIDUAL ACTIVITY

Read the following poem taken from an anti-bullying campaign then answer the questions that follow.

I AM

by Laura

I am the person you bullied at school
I am the person who didn't know how to be cool
I am the person that you alienated
I am the person you ridiculed and hated
I am the person who sat on her own
I am the person who walked home alone
I am the person you scared every day
I am the person who had nothing to say
I am the person with hurt in his eyes
I am the person you never saw cry
I am the person living alone with his fears
I am the person destroyed by his peers
I am the person you drowned in your scorn
I am the person who wished she hadn't been born
I am the person you destroyed for fun
I am the person but not the only one
I am the person whose name you didn't know
I am the person who just can't let go
I am the person who has feelings too
I am a person, just like you.

1. How did this poem make you feel?

_____

2. How does the poem make you feel about the person being bullied?

_____

3. How do you think the person being bullied feels?

_____

4. What are your feelings towards the bully?

_____

5. How do you think the bully would feel after reading this poem?

_____

6. What advice would you give to this person if you knew them?

_____

7. What advice would you give to the bully?

_____

INDIVIDUAL ACTIVITY

Using the poem 'I Am' as an example, write two verses of a positive poem about the person who stops to help. The poem has been started for you.

> I am the person who stopped the fight
> I am the person who knew it wasn't right
> I am the person who _____
> I am the person who _____
>
> I am the person who _____
> I am the person who _____
> I am the person who _____
> And I am the person who _____

 Go to YouTube and search for 'Bystanders Can Make a Difference – Student Video – Hey UGLY' (7.00).

REFLECTION ON MY LEARNING

Circle of Support

Working in small groups, write one action each person or group could do to stand up or tackle the issue of bullying in the circles on the right.

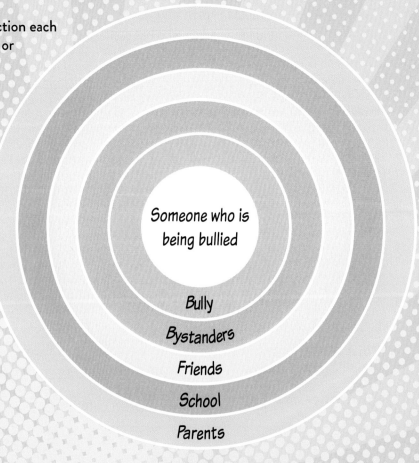

Someone who is being bullied

Bully

Bystanders

Friends

School

Parents

LESSON 11

Cyberbullying and Online Abusive Behaviour

Learning Outcomes: 4.4, 4.6, 4.7, 4.8

responsible   resilient   respected   aware

By the end of this lesson, you will:

- recognise what cyberbullying and online abusive behaviour is
- understand the importance of being an upstander in situations of online bullying
- identify the barriers to standing up to online abusive behaviour and bullying.

KEYWORDS

Cyberbullying
Online abusive behaviour

ADDITIONAL RESOURCES

www.tacklebullying.ie A national website to help young people, parents and teachers counter bullying and cyberbullying.

www.webwise.ie Webwise is an Irish internet safety awareness centre. This website has a youth section which provides tips and advice on bullying and cyberbullying.

www.barnardos.ie Provides information and advice on how to deal with bullying.

What are Cyberbullying and Online Abusive Behaviour?

INDIVIDUAL ACTIVITY

In your opinion, what is cyberbullying?	What does online abusive behaviour look like?

69

For most people, the internet is a positive and fun and useful tool. It allows us to connect with others and share memories, and gives us a platform to express our opinions. However, some people use social media for the wrong reasons, as a way of bullying, intimidating or harassing others. Cyberbullying and other forms of online abusive behaviour can happen to anyone at any time and can cause huge distress. Cyberbullying is particularly hard to deal with compared to other forms of bullying because it leaves the person feeling there is no safe place to get away from the bully. Imagine what it would feel like when, every time you go online, you have to face unkind comments and criticism, threatening or aggressive messages. A person who is cyberbullied may feel isolated and unsure how to stop it happening to them. The important thing to remember is that there are ways of dealing and coping with cyberbullying. In this lesson, we will examine different types of cyberbullying and how to stand up to online bullying.

> Posting a one-off offensive message online about someone is cyberbullying, as it can be copied and shared with thousands of people.

Go to YouTube and search 'Talent Show Cyberbullying Prevention Commercial' (0:50) to watch a video that was made to raise awareness of cyberbullying.

CLASS DISCUSSION

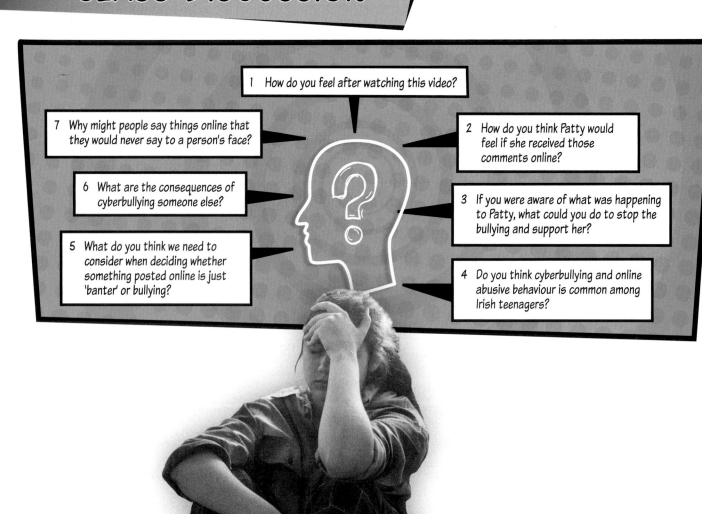

1 How do you feel after watching this video?

2 How do you think Patty would feel if she received those comments online?

3 If you were aware of what was happening to Patty, what could you do to stop the bullying and support her?

4 Do you think cyberbullying and online abusive behaviour is common among Irish teenagers?

5 What do you think we need to consider when deciding whether something posted online is just 'banter' or bullying?

6 What are the consequences of cyberbullying someone else?

7 Why might people say things online that they would never say to a person's face?

Cyberbullying and Irish Teenagers

A recent survey of 5,000 young people from 11 different countries found that Irish teens are bullied online more than teenagers in other countries.

28% of Irish teenagers said they were bullied online.

TWO-THIRDS of Irish teenagers feel cyberbullying is worse than face-to-face bullying.

OVER HALF of Irish teenagers felt that cyberbullying is more of an issue than drug abuse.

45% of Irish teens feel helpless when they are victims of cyberbullying.

26% were upset or scared by something they witnessed online.

29% stated they feel 'completely alone' after been cyberbullied.

9 out of **10** Irish teens said that they would find coping with cyberbullying easier if they received support from friends online at the time of the bullying.

#%@!$

LOSER

71

Types of Cyberbullying and Online Abusive Behaviour

Personal intimidation

Sending nasty, mean, abusive or threatening comments, videos, emails or photos to a person, causing fear for the person. These can be sent to a person's messaging app, email account or social media page.

Impersonation

Pretending to be someone else by setting up fake profiles or web pages in another person's name, or accessing someone's social media profile or messaging apps and sending material intending to get the person in trouble.

Exclusion

Deliberately and cruelly blocking or removing someone from an online messaging group or platform.

Personal humiliation

Posting images, videos or comments online with the intention of embarrassing someone.

False reporting

Making false complaints to the online service provider or reporting other users with a view to having the user's account deleted.

Cyberstalking

Is when someone harasses or stalks a person using electronic devices. It involves repeatedly sending unwanted messages or making phone calls repeatedly to another person. Repeatedly harassing a person or posting hurtful or belittling messages online directed at them.

INDIVIDUAL ACTIVITY

Look at the scenarios below and identify the type(s) of cyberbullying that is taking place in each case.

	Scenario	Type(s) of bullying
1.	Caolan is being bullied by a group of students in his school. Every time he accesses his social media, he faces unkind comments and threatening messages.	
2.	A group of girls have taken a dislike to their Geography teacher. They found a picture of him online and created a fake social media account in his name. They post rumours and spiteful comments about the teacher on the page.	
3.	When Rachel broke up with Jakub, he repeatedly sent her messages telling her that he didn't want them to break up and that he cannot cope without her. He continues to message her every day, even though she has asked him to stop. Some of his messages can get nasty.	
4.	Natalie's friend group in school have started being really off with her. She recently got on the wrong side of one of the girls. When Natalie checked her Snapchat, she found that she was blocked from the group.	
5.	Lin and her friends are hanging out at her house. Lin goes to the kitchen to make tea but leaves Instagram open on her phone. Her friends decide it would be funny to send a message to Mark – a guy Lin really likes – and tell him that she fancies him.	
6.	Alex gets teased a bit at school, but he tries to laugh it off and show that it doesn't bother him that much. Recently, however, it has got worse. After PE class, Matt took a picture of Alex undressing and sent it to other students in the school.	
7.	John shared a nude with Lisa. She shared it with others.	
8.	Tom loves making YouTube videos of himself reviewing online games. He checks the comments and notices a few horrible ones calling him 'loser' and telling him to 'get a life'. He also finds a video of someone mimicking him.	
9.	Devi and Hannah love gaming, and they connect with lots of friends online. Recently another player seems to have been targeting them and purposely killing off their characters at the start of the game. Devi and Hannah have also started to receive threatening messages while playing. When they try to block this player, they keep showing up under a different username.	

WHAT TO DO IF YOU ARE BEING CYBERBULLIED OR HARASSED ONLINE

BREAK THE SILENCE
Tell someone you trust and get support. This could be a parent, a teacher or a trusted adult.

CONTACT THE GARDAÍ
If the bullying persists, contact the Gardaí. www.hotline.ie is an anonymous helpline for reporting any illegal content shared online.

KEEP THE EVIDENCE
Screenshot the messages or pages. Keep a record of the dates and times. This will help to keep track of the extent of the bullying.

BLOCK THE PERSON
Most social media platforms have a 'block' function. Use it to help prevent further bullying from taking place.

DON'T RESPOND
Even if you want to, don't reply to the bullying message. Responding can encourage the bully and make the situation worse, as they may want you to react.

REPORT THE BULLYING
In most sites and apps, you can report abusive or inappropriate messages. Use these systems to log a complaint online or to report bullying messages.

The Bystander Effect

In the previous lesson, you learned about the 'bystander effect' in real-world incidences of bullying. The bystander effect means that often the more people who see something happen, the less likely each individual is to do something about it. This is true in online incidences of bullying, too.

Go to YouTube and search 'The Bystander Effect WatchYourSpace' (1:43) to watch a video about the bystander effect in online settings.

GROUP ACTIVITY

Barriers to Standing Up to Cyberbullying

In your small groups, discuss and write down some of the reasons young people may not intervene when they are aware of or witness online bullying.

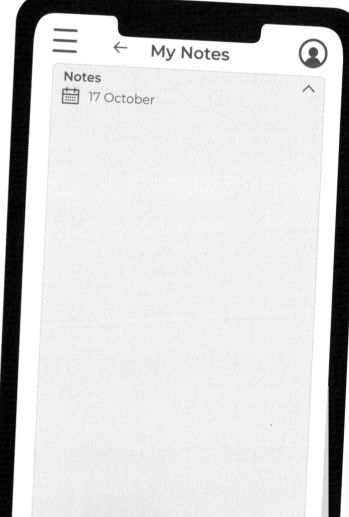

Be an Upstander, Not a Bystander

Bullying is everyone's business – we all have a role to play in protecting each other against online harassment and cyberbullying. It won't go away however much we ignore it. Below are some steps you can take to be an upstander, not a bystander.

- Decide first whether the action is harmless or hurtful. Don't join in or share any comments, posts or pictures that may hurt others.

- Tell a trusted adult what you see.

- Let the person being bullied know that you support them.

- Put yourself in the other person's shoes and imagine how they are feeling.

- Tell them about organisations or people in the school that could help them.

- Act quickly. Online bullying can get out of control quickly and it can be overwhelming for the person affected.

- Report any incidences of cyberbullying you observe to the app or service provider.

- Screengrab and save any offensive or abusive messages to report it to the app or service provider.

- Don't bully the bully. It's OK to point out that the cyberbullying or harassment should stop, but sending abusive messages back won't help anyone.

- Don't support cyberbullies or be encouraged by them to exclude or harass someone.

- Do not post comments you would not say in public or face to face.

Showing Respect and Empathy for Others Online

Sometimes, people who bully do not realise the harmful impact of their actions. They may think that what they are doing is a harmless joke.

Sometimes people who bully do it because they do not feel good about themselves, or are going through difficulties, and bullying others can make them feel better about themselves.

People sometimes join in with bullying behaviour because they go along with what others are doing.

Always be mindful of the person who would be receiving the comment and put yourself in their shoes. Never post something online that you wouldn't say to a person's face. A great tip for helping you decide what you should say online is to use the THINK acronym:

THINK

T = Is it **True**?

H = Is it **Helpful**?

I = Is it **Illegal**?

N = Is it **Necessary**?

K = Is it **Kind**?

Empathy and Respect Online

Gather into small groups. Your teacher will assign you one of the scenarios below.
Read the scenario and answer the questions that follow.

1. You see a comment that a friend has made about someone else on TikTok. You think it is funny, but it might be taken the wrong way and hurt the person's feelings.

2. You see a person being body-shamed on Instagram. You don't know the person, but a lot of people are joining in with hurtful comments.

3. While chatting with your friends in your WhatsApp group, one friend starts to talk about another girl in your class, saying very mean things about her.

4. You discover that someone has created a fake TikTok account impersonating a boy in your year and making nasty comments about him.

5. A nude picture of a girl in your year is circulating. Even though you haven't asked for it, one of your friends has sent it to you.

6. Your friend has sent you a funny video of someone in your year group falling over. Your friend is telling you to share it, that it is only a laugh.

What should you do in this situation?

_____

_____

_____

Why should you do it?

_____

_____

_____

How could you do it?

_____

_____

_____

How would you feel if you were at the receiving end of this post?

_____

_____

_____

REFLECTION ON MY LEARNING

Three things I have learned about cyberbullying and online harassment are:

1. _____

2. _____

3. _____

If I witnessed or was aware of someone being cyberbullied, I would:

_____

_____

RESPECTFUL COMMUNICATION ONLINE AND OFFLINE

LESSON 12

Effective Communication

Learning Outcome: 1.7

connected   respected   aware

By the end of this lesson, you will:

•• appreciate the role of words, body language and tone in respectful and effective communication.

KEYWORDS

Communication
Body language
Tone
Listening
Respectful communication
Effective communication
Verbal communication
Non-verbal communication

ADDITIONAL RESOURCES

www.reachout.com Provides information on effective communication and good listening skills.

PAIR ACTIVITY

Draw Me a Picture

Step 1: Decide who will be A and who will be B.

Step 2: Sit back to back.

Step 3: A draws a simple picture into the frame on the facing page, using only shapes and lines, similar to the example given on the right. B cannot look while A is drawing their picture.

Step 4: When A has finished drawing their picture, they cover it up. They then give Person B oral instructions on how to draw the picture, which they draw into the other frame. Person A must not look at Person B's work while they are drawing. Person B must not ask any questions.

Step 5: When B has finished, compare the drawings.

Step 6: Switch roles.

Person A drawing

Person B drawing

CLASS DISCUSSION

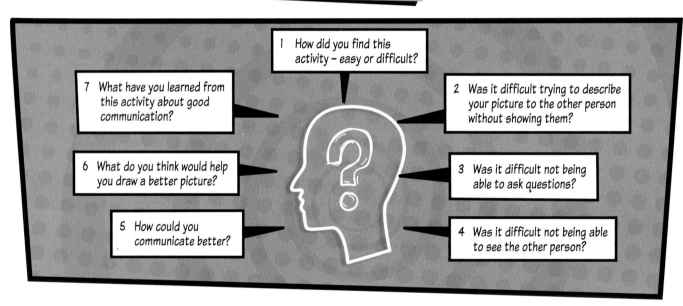

1   How did you find this activity – easy or difficult?

7   What have you learned from this activity about good communication?

2   Was it difficult trying to describe your picture to the other person without showing them?

6   What do you think would help you draw a better picture?

3   Was it difficult not being able to ask questions?

5   How could you communicate better?

4   Was it difficult not being able to see the other person?

How Do We Communicate?

Communication is not just about the words we speak – tone of voice and body language also play a role in how we get the message we want across to others.

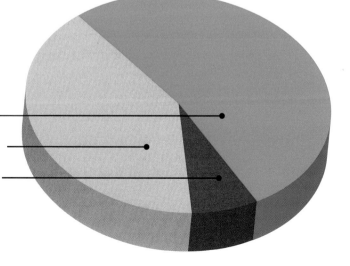

55% = body language

38% = tone (How we say it)

7% = verbal (What we say)

Tone of Voice

Many words, sentences and phrases have different meanings depending on the tone in which they are said and the words that are stressed. Your tone of voice can greatly influence how a message is received by others. It is not about what you say, more about how you say it.

Sometimes we need to check the tone of voice we are using to ensure we are getting the right message across. It is for that reason that text messages can sometimes be misinterpreted as you cannot 'hear' a tone of voice when you read it. For example, a phrase like 'That's a great idea' said with an enthusiastic tone demonstrates genuine excitement for the idea, but if it is said using a sarcastic tone, it may convey that the idea is not that great. (Emojis can express intention, but they're not always reliable!)

PAIR ACTIVITY

1. In pairs, practise saying the following sentence in three different tones.

What do you want?

What do you want?

What do you want?

2. Now, make up two more sentences where stressing different words changes the meaning. Write the examples you come up with below:

Sentence 1: _____

Sentence 2: _____

3. What is the main thing you learned from doing this exercise?

_____

_____

Body Language

As you saw in the pie chart, body language makes up the largest part of how we communicate with others and what messages they receive from us. Body language is how we communicate non-verbally, where we use our bodies to convey our message. Body language often reveals our true feelings or emotions, and gives out positive or negative messages to others depending on how we use it. We can be aware that we are using body language to convey our meaning, but sometimes we use body language unintentionally.

Types of Body Language

Ways of talking (e.g. pauses, stress on words)

Posture (e.g. slouching)

Appearance (e.g. untidiness)

Head movements (e.g. nodding)

Hand movements (e.g. waving)

Eye movements (e.g. winking)

Facial expressions (e.g. frowning)

Body contact (e.g. shaking hands)

Closeness (e.g. invading someone else's space)

Sounds (e.g. laughing)

Sensitive and Respectful Communication

THINK

T = Is it **T**rue?

H = Is it **H**elpful?

I = Is it **I**llegal?

N = Is it **N**ecessary?

K = Is it **K**ind?

Verbal communication

Choose your words carefully:

- Although they are not the whole story, they are important.
- Consider how what you say could impact on others.
- Speak in a way that shows understanding and respect for others.
  - You can use the acronym THINK before you speak.

Non-verbal communication

Be aware of your body language

- Show the other person you are interested in what they are saying.
- Is your body language showing respect? Have an open, approachable stance. Keep your arms uncrossed and avoid fidgeting or sitting rigidly.
- Respect personal space. Be mindful of how close you are to the other person.

Be aware of your facial expressions

- Our facial expressions can tell a lot about how we and others are feeling. Use appropriate facial expressions to show interest in the other person.
- Smiling can show friendliness and warmth.
- Maintaining eye contact is another way of showing respect and interest in the other person.

Take care with your tone

- Be aware of how you say what you say.
- Make sure your tone of voice is calm and respectful.

Go to YouTube and search for 'Non-verbal communication game' (1:51) and answer the questions posed.

 Go to YouTube and search for 'Quiz on Facial Expressions | microexpressions | body language: How Well Can You Read People?' (6:07) and answer the questions posed.

INDIVIDUAL ACTIVITY

What are the potential barriers to respectful and effective communication in an online setting?

_____

_____

_____

REFLECTION ON MY LEARNING

Three ways I can show respect when communicating with others are:

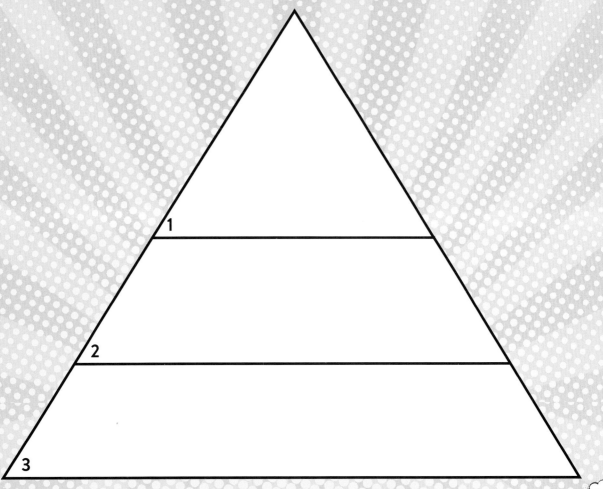

1

2

3

LESSON 13
Effective and Respectful Listening

Learning Outcome: 1.7

connected · respected · responsible

By the end of this lesson, you will:

➻ know what it means to listen openly and sensitively to the views and feelings of others

➻ have practised the skills for effective listening.

KEYWORDS

Listening skills
Selective listening

ADDITIONAL RESOURCES

www.reachout.com Provides information on effective communication and good listening skills.

Listen Up

Listening is a two-way process: sometimes we will be the speaker and sometimes we will be the listener. Listening is a very important skill that not everyone has, but it can be improved.

Being a good listener is not just about listening to the words a person is speaking – it is about giving them your full attention and really trying to understand what they are saying. Being a good listener helps us to get along better with the people in our lives and build meaningful connections. When we listen attentively to others, it shows that we care about them and that we are genuinely interested in what they are saying.

Good listening skills can also help to resolve disagreements in our lives. When we take time to listen carefully to a person, it allows us to see things from their point of view and why they might feel the way they do.

INDIVIDUAL ACTIVITY

Rate My Listening

How well do you listen to others? Mark on the scale to the right how well you think you listen to others.

PAIR ACTIVITY

In pairs, complete the three activities below. After each activity, discuss the questions that follow as a class.

Listening Game 1: Face to Face

Instructions:

Step 1: Sit on chairs facing each other.

Step 2: When the teacher gives the signal, speak to each other for 30 seconds at the same time about what you did last weekend.

Listening Game 2: Back to Back

Instructions:

Step 1: Decide who will be A and who will be B.

Step 2: Sit back to back.

Step 3: When the teacher gives the signal, A talks to B for 30 seconds about what they like to do in their free time.

Step 4: Switch roles.

Listening Game 3: Not Listening

Instructions:

Step 1: Decide who will be A and who will be B.

Step 2: Sit on chairs facing each other.

Step 3: When the teacher gives the signal, A talks to B about their favourite movie. B must act as if they're not listening to A at all.

Step 4: Switch roles.

85

CLASS DISCUSSION

1 What did it feel like doing that activity?

2 Was it difficult to hear your partner?

3 What affected your ability to listen to the other person?

4 What is the main message you got about good listening from doing this activity?

Listening Quiz

The quiz below will help you determine the type of listener you are. Read the following 10 statements about listening below and select the response that best represents your behaviour when listening to others.

STATEMENT	Always	Often	Sometimes	Rarely	Never
1. When others are speaking, I interrupt them to try to get my point across.					
2. I switch off and stop listening to the other person if what they are speaking about doesn't interest me.					
3. I am easily distracted by my phone when others are speaking to me.					
4. At times, I find myself drifting off in a daydream when people are talking to me.					
5. How much I like a person influences how much I listen to them.					
6. I find it difficult to maintain eye contact when someone is speaking to me.					
7. When someone is speaking, I tend to not listen to them and want them to hurry up so I can speak.					
8. I find myself finishing other people's sentences.					
9. I sometimes stop listening but use words to pretend I am still listening, like 'yeah', 'uh huh', 'I know'.					
10. I find it difficult to listen to someone I disagree with.					

Scoring

Always: 1 point
Often: 2 points
Sometimes: 3 points
Rarely: 4 points
Never: 5 points

Add up your score for all 10 questions to determine how good a listener you are.

1–10 points: Unfortunately, you are a poor listener. You need to work on your listening skills.

11–20 points: Your listening skills need some improvement.

21–30 points: You are a fair listener.

31–40 points: You are a good listener.

41–50 points: Well done! You are an excellent listener.

How to Be a Respectful Listener

Give your full attention

When you are in a conversation with someone, avoid distractions. Don't look at your phone, even if you're bored. This can give the message that you are more interested in your phone than what the person has to say.

Show interest

Show the other person that you are interested in what they are saying. Maintain good eye contact, use body language like nodding your head, smiling and leaning forward to show you are listening.

Ask questions

Ask questions to show that you are interested in learning more about what the person is saying. Use open-ended questions as these encourage people to share more. These are questions that can't be answered with a simple 'yes' or 'no'. For example, 'How did you feel then?', 'Why do you think that?', 'What did you do?'

Offer verbal cues

Show the speaker you are listening with your words. This can be done with verbal cues like 'I agree with you', 'I see', 'Really?', 'That's interesting', 'That's great'.

Avoid interrupting

Don't interrupt the other person when they are speaking. Be patient – give them time to finish what they are saying. Don't rush in with your own points and avoid finishing their sentences.

Avoid giving too much advice

Try not to talk too much. Don't hog the conversation with your advice and opinions. Only give advice if it is asked for.

Five Poor Listening Habits

1 **Spacing out** – this is when someone is talking to you and your mind starts to wander. You are caught up in your own thoughts.

Yeah, that's great ...

I broke my leg!

2 **Pretend listening** – when you pretend you are paying attention by using sympathetic words/sounds such as 'yeah', 'uh huh', 'I know'.

3 **Selective listening** – when you only pay attention to the part of the conversation that you are interested in.

Wait until I tell you about my last trip to the dentist

My tooth hurts so badly

Lucky you, missing school

I missed school because my Gran is very ill

4 **Word listening** – when you do not pick up the clues about how the person is feeling, only the words they say. You do not notice the other person's body language or tone of voice.

As soon as he stops going on, I'll tell him about what happened to me on Friday night

5 **Self-centred listening** – when you are waiting for the other person to finish talking so that you can speak. You are more interested in telling your story than hearing what they have to say.

INDIVIDUAL ACTIVITY

Your teacher will choose two people to role-play the following dialogue between Martin and Ivan. When the role play is finished, identify the poor communication and listening habits displayed.

Martin and Ivan

Martin and Ivan are friends. Martin meets Ivan on his own after school.

Martin	*(upbeat, looking down at his phone)* Hey, Ivan! How's things?
Ivan	*(downbeat)* Hey. All right.
Martin	*(briefly looking up from his phone)* What's up with you?
Ivan	*(defeated but not wanting to reveal too much)* Nothing much … I didn't get picked for the team.
Martin	*(excitedly, looking up from his phone)* Oh, actually, did I tell you – I made captain! I can't wait for the match. I think we've a very strong chance this year …
Ivan	*(now getting angry)* Yeah, well, that doesn't mean much to me because I won't be on the team.
Martin	*(cutting off Ivan, distractedly)* Yeah? Oh well, that's too bad …
Ivan	To make matters worse, we were meant to be going over to Old Trafford next month for my birthday, but we can't now because …
Martin	Talking of trips, I can't wait for the adventure centre trip!
Ivan	I can't go to that … I can't be asking my parents for money for trips like that these days because …
Martin	You're joking! All the lads are going. Try to get around them – it'll be great. Anyhow, I'll be putting photos up so you can see all the craic there if you can't go.
Ivan	Right … Talk to you later.
Martin	Yeah, see you later. And hey, cheer up before then!

REFLECTION ON MY LEARNING

Having completed this lesson, write below what you think effective listening looks likes, sounds like and feels like.

Looks like 👁	Sounds like 👂	Feels like ♥

89

LESSON 14 — Passive, Aggressive and Assertive Communication

Learning Outcome: 1.7

 respected connected responsible

By the end of this lesson, you will:

• understand three main styles of communication

• appreciate what respectful communication means

• demonstrate how to communicate in a respectful and effective way.

KEYWORDS

Passive communication
Aggressive communication
Assertive communication

ADDITIONAL RESOURCES

www.reachout.com Provides information on effective communication and good listening skills.

www.kidshealth.org Search 'assertive' for information on assertive communication for teens.

Communication Styles

We generally communicate in three different styles.

The Assertiveness Scale

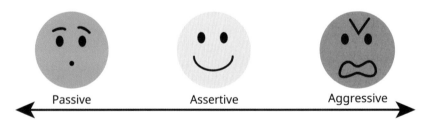

Passive   Assertive   Aggressive

The communication style we use can depend on the situation we are in and the people we are communicating with. For example, we may have no problem standing up to our siblings, but may struggle saying how we feel to our friends.

Whether it is expressing your opinion, standing up for yourself or saying no to a request, understanding the different communication styles will help you express your thoughts and feelings more effectively while respecting the rights of others.

Passive Communication

When a person uses this communication style, they do not say how they really feel or what they really want. They put other people's wants and feelings before their own, sometimes to avoid arguments. They often agree to things they don't want to, with the result that they don't get what they need or want and sometimes feel resentful.

Verbal Clues

- Stay silent and don't express their opinion
- Apologise excessively
- Speak softly or hesitantly

Body Language

- Avoid eye contact
- Slouched shoulders
- Nervous or fidgety
- Crossed arms

Aggressive Communication

When a person uses this communication style, they try to get what they want by bullying or disrespecting others. They want their own way, usually at the expense of others. They put their own rights and feelings before others'. It often leads to conflict or bad feelings.

Verbal Clues

- Raised voice
- Forceful tone
- Interrupting others
- Using insults or criticism

Body Language

- Stare people down
- Invade personal space
- Intense facial expressions
- Point fingers

Assertive Communication

When a person uses this style of communication, they express their feelings honestly and confidently while also respecting others. They stand up for themselves and their rights. They resolve conflicts in a respectful manner. People respect this style of communication as they know where they stand and appreciate honesty.

Verbal Clues

- Say what they feel
- Speak calmly
- Use 'I' statements

Body Language

- Open, relaxed posture
- Listen attentively
- Stand straight and upright
- Maintain eye contact

Appropriate Communication: Reading the Situation

Assertive communication is an effective style in most situations. However, sometimes we may have to 'read' the situation and decide what the most suitable communication style to use is. There may be a situation where we have to be sensitive to the other person's feelings. For example, if your dad has put a lot of effort into preparing dinner and you don't like it, it is not a good idea to tell him exactly how you feel, as you may hurt his feelings.

A passive response may also be the best option to prevent potentially dangerous situations getting worse for us.

Using assertive communication while having respect for others does not mean we will always get what we want, and we may have to agree to disagree in some situations.

CLASS DISCUSSION

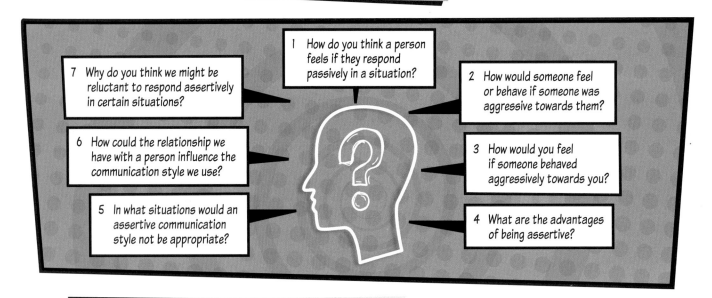

7 Why do you think we might be reluctant to respond assertively in certain situations?

6 How could the relationship we have with a person influence the communication style we use?

5 In what situations would an assertive communication style not be appropriate?

1 How do you think a person feels if they respond passively in a situation?

2 How would someone feel or behave if someone was aggressive towards them?

3 How would you feel if someone behaved aggressively towards you?

4 What are the advantages of being assertive?

INDIVIDUAL ACTIVITY

Read the five scenarios below and write down how you could respond assertively.

Scenario 1

Your sibling is always taking your clothes without permission.

Scenario 2

You order at a restaurant, but it is lukewarm. You call the waiter over.

Scenario 3

You are working on your Science CBA in a group, and one of your classmates is not doing any work.

Scenario 4

Your friend keeps asking you to borrow your Maths homework, and you are tired of it.

Scenario 5

Your classmate keeps talking to you during English class, and you are getting in trouble.

Tips for Assertive Communication

Stay calm: Breathe normally, maintain eye contact, keep your face relaxed and speak with a relaxed tone.

Use 'I' statements: Stick to statements that begin with 'I', such as 'I think' or 'I feel'. Avoid using aggressive language such as 'You always' or 'You never'.

Use repetition: Repeat your message quietly but firmly, paying attention to your body language and tone of voice.

Be prepared: If you think the conversation will be difficult, have a line ready for what you want to say and rehearse it beforehand.

Stick to the point: Don't be drawn into disagreements that have nothing to do with the issue.

Be patient: Being assertive is a skill that needs practice – you may not get it right all the time.

Listen: Listen to the other person's point of view, use active listening skills you have learned.

Show respect: Always show respect for the other person's point of view even though you may not agree with it.

Find a 'win-win': Try to reach a compromise where both people's needs are met.

Be confident: Stand tall, make eye contact.

GROUP ACTIVITY

What are some of the potential barriers to assertive communication? Discuss in your small groups.

Role Play

Below are situations where a young person may have to demonstrate assertiveness. Select one situation and create a dialogue that shows an assertive response in that situation. If you feel comfortable, you can role-play it.

1. Asking a friend to return something they borrowed

2. Telling a group of friends that you don't want to participate in something they are doing

3. Saying 'no' to a request that goes against your values

4. Requesting to be treated fairly in a situation you feel you have been treated unfairly

5. Expressing your feelings when you feel hurt or annoyed

6. Giving someone a compliment

7. Starting a conversation with someone you don't know

8. Making a complaint

REFLECTION ON MY LEARNING

It can be difficult to be assertive sometimes, and some situations are more difficult than others.

A situation I would find difficult to be assertive in is _____

_____

The reason for this is _____

_____

I can work on becoming more assertive in this situation by _____

_____

_____

LESSON 15 — Responsible Online Sharing

Learning Outcomes: 2.7, 2.8, 2.9

 connected
 responsible
 aware

By the end of this lesson, you will:

- assess the benefits and challenges of your online world
- discuss how to share personal information, images, opinions and emotions in a safe, responsible manner online
- explore the risks of sharing intimate images online.

KEYWORDS

Online sharing
Sexting
Intimate images

ADDITIONAL RESOURCES

www.tacklebullying.ie A national website providing help and resources for young people, parents and teachers to counter bullying and cyberbullying.

www.webwise.ie Webwise is the national Irish Internet Safety Awareness Centre. This website has a youth section which provides tips and advice on bullying and cyberbullying.

www.barnardos.ie Provides information and advice on how to deal with bullying.

Our online world can be a great place to have fun and connect with others. Through social media posts, comments, videos, we can stay in touch with friends, family and classmates with just the click of a button. However, we need to think responsibly about what we share online – and who we share it with. We need to be aware that the content and information we share online can have repercussions and negative consequences for us and others.

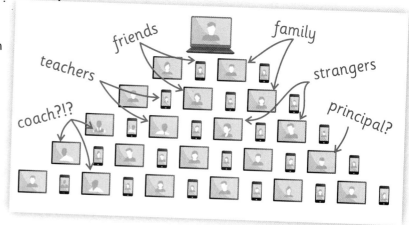

What we share now can come back to haunt us in the future. What we post can be easily copied and shared by other internet users. Once something is shared online, we have no control over where it can go.

Other people's impressions of us can also be influenced by what we share, so it is so important to create a positive impression of ourselves online. In this lesson, we will look at the benefits and challenges of our online world. You will also learn how to share information, images, opinions and emotions in a safe and responsible manner online.

How we Connect Online

CLASS ACTIVITY

There are many different ways we connect online.

You will now take part in a class survey to determine the different apps and platforms people in your class use to connect online. Your teacher will call out the method of online communication from the bar chart. Raise your hand if you use that method/app. Count the number of people with hands up, and record the number in the table below. Use the information to complete the bar chart.

Method of connection	Snapchat	Instagram	Email	Online gaming	WhatsApp	Twitter	TikTok	YouTube	Other
No. of students									

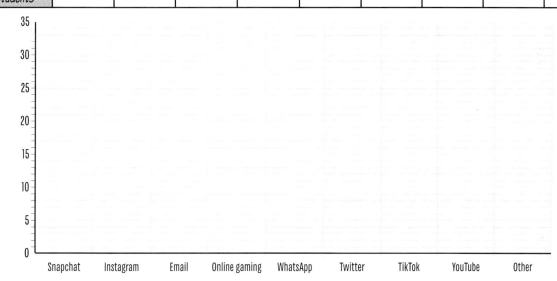

CLASS DISCUSSION

1 What do you enjoy about connecting with others online?

10 Do people feel more comfortable doing or saying things online than in person? Why?

2 What role do group chats play in friendships?

9 Can what we share online be misinterpreted? How?

3 Do you think young people spend too much time online?

8 How would you know if you are spending too much time online?

4 What do you think is OK to share online?

7 What could be the negative consequences of online sharing?

5 What do you think is not OK to share online?

6 What are the positive aspects of online sharing?

Benefits and Challenges of Our Online World

GROUP ACTIVITY

In the table below, write down what you think the benefits and challenges of engaging in the online world are for young people.

BENEFITS	CHALLENGES

GROUP ACTIVITY

Your teacher will assign each group one of the scenarios below. Read and discuss the scenario, then answer the question.

Scenario 1

It is 7.30 p.m. Molly is meant to be meeting her friend Joe to go to the cinema at 8 p.m. Molly is tired and doesn't feel like it any more. She thinks the best thing to do is send Joe a text to cancel.

What should Molly think about before sending the text?

Scenario 2

Tom is at the beach. He sees someone getting into difficulty in the water and the lifeguards going to rescue them. Tom decides to record the event and thinks about posting it online.

What advice would you give Tom?

Scenario 3

Sofia is online and sees a video that was shared of her friend Cara tripping in the school show. People are writing comments underneath mocking Cara. Sofia thinks it would be a bit of fun to join in.

What does Sofia need to think about before doing this?

Scenario 4

Allie is a big hurling fan and proud Limerick girl. She loves Limerick, but she thinks one of the players has been playing poorly and shouldn't be picked for the next game. She goes on Twitter and sees a tweet that says, '[The player] is so rubbish, I don't know how he is getting his place on the team.' Allie thinks about replying to this tweet with her opinion on the player.

What advice would you give Allie?

Scenario 5

Cal loves soccer and never misses a training session. The coach has always said many times that if you don't show up to training, you won't be allowed to play. At the last match, the coach started a player who rarely shows up to training. The next training is after school tomorrow. Cal feels the best thing to do is email the coach and say he is going to give up soccer.

What should Cal do?

Scenario 6

Katia is having a bad day. She got into trouble in school, and she is sick of her parents arguing. She goes online and posts about how she is feeling.

What does Katia need to think about before posting?

Scenario 7

Em and Sarah Louise are enjoying their summer holidays. One particular hot day, they decide to go to their local swimming pool. While at the pool, they practise their diving. Sarah Louise asks Em to record her diving so she sees how she looks. Sarah Louise dives into the water, but when she resurfaces her bikini top has fallen off. Em has got it all on video and thinks it would be very funny to share it on their friend group's WhatsApp.

What does Em need to think about before sharing this post?

Before you post or share online:
STOP THINK CHOOSE

What we post online can have many repercussions for us and for others. It is important to stop and think before we choose what to do.

99

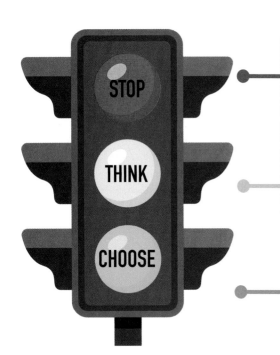

Before you post ...

Calm down and take a few deep breaths before responding. Ask yourself: 'Is it wise to post this now? Am I posting this in anger? Am I calm enough to send this now?'

What could be the consequences of me responding in this way? Is there a better way of communicating how I feel? Could I hurt someone's feelings? Would I be happy if it went viral? Am I giving a good impression of myself? How would I feel if I received this message? Am I sharing personal information?

Choose the best option: delete or post. Talk to someone you trust for support if you are concerned.

INDIVIDUAL ACTIVITY

 Go to YouTube and search for 'Teach students about posting publicly or privately online' (3:36).

 Go to YouTube and search for 'Oversharing: Think Before You Post' (3:35)

Using what you have learned from the videos and from class so far, write three important messages you think young people your age should know about online sharing.

Think Before You Click: Things to Remember When You Post Online

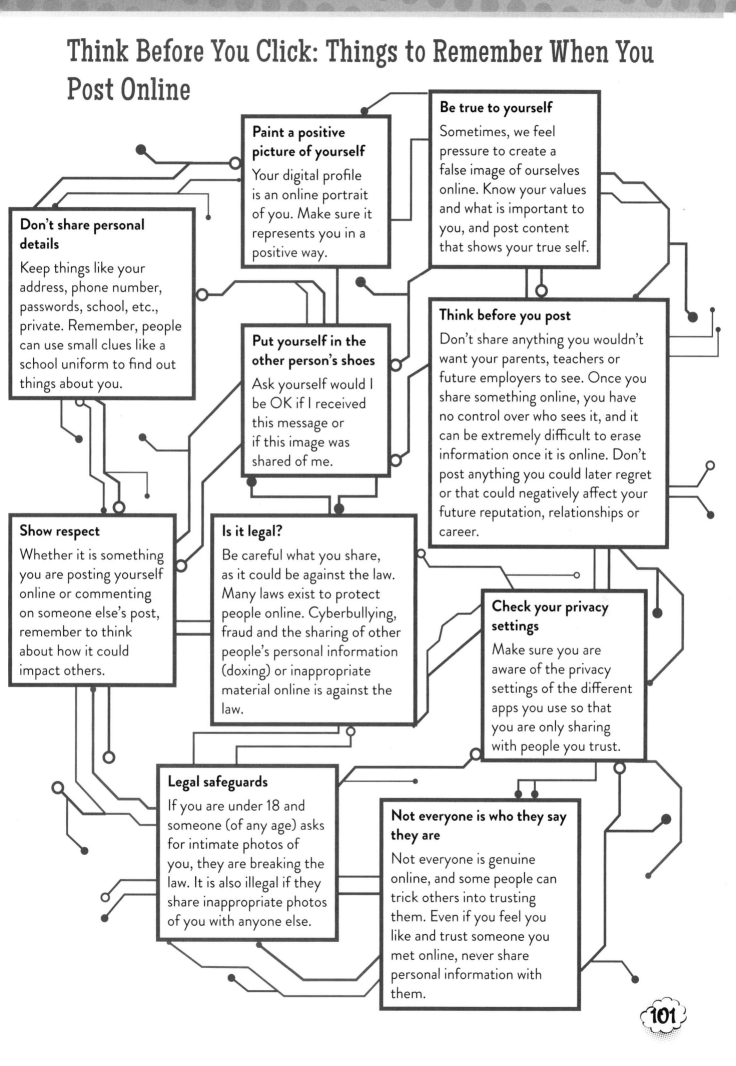

Paint a positive picture of yourself

Your digital profile is an online portrait of you. Make sure it represents you in a positive way.

Be true to yourself

Sometimes, we feel pressure to create a false image of ourselves online. Know your values and what is important to you, and post content that shows your true self.

Don't share personal details

Keep things like your address, phone number, passwords, school, etc., private. Remember, people can use small clues like a school uniform to find out things about you.

Think before you post

Don't share anything you wouldn't want your parents, teachers or future employers to see. Once you share something online, you have no control over who sees it, and it can be extremely difficult to erase information once it is online. Don't post anything you could later regret or that could negatively affect your future reputation, relationships or career.

Put yourself in the other person's shoes

Ask yourself would I be OK if I received this message or if this image was shared of me.

Show respect

Whether it is something you are posting yourself online or commenting on someone else's post, remember to think about how it could impact others.

Is it legal?

Be careful what you share, as it could be against the law. Many laws exist to protect people online. Cyberbullying, fraud and the sharing of other people's personal information (doxing) or inappropriate material online is against the law.

Check your privacy settings

Make sure you are aware of the privacy settings of the different apps you use so that you are only sharing with people you trust.

Legal safeguards

If you are under 18 and someone (of any age) asks for intimate photos of you, they are breaking the law. It is also illegal if they share inappropriate photos of you with anyone else.

Not everyone is who they say they are

Not everyone is genuine online, and some people can trick others into trusting them. Even if you feel you like and trust someone you met online, never share personal information with them.

Online Sharing: Laws You Should Know

Coco's Law

Under the Harassment, Harmful Communications and Related Offences Act 2021, known as Coco's Law, it is illegal to send, receive or share intimate (nude) images, video or text of someone else, without consent. This law applies whether you are under or over 18.

Under Coco's Law, it is also an offence to send or share any 'threatening or grossly offensive communication'. This means that under this law, cyberbullying, harassing, inciting hatred against, impersonating or defaming a person is against the law. The law applies to all types of communication both online and offline.

Criminal Law (Sexual Offences) Act 2017 and Child Trafficking and Pornography Act 1998

Under these laws it is illegal to send, receive or share an explicit (nude) image, video or text of a child, under 18. It is also an offence to cause a child to watch sexual activity.

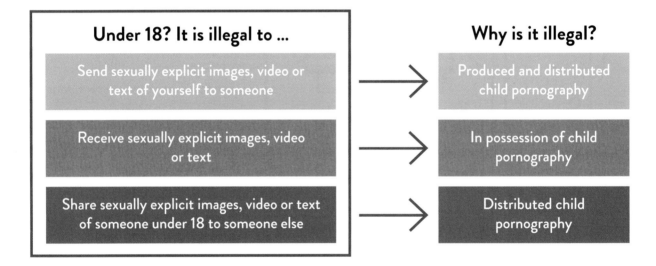

GDPR Law

Under General Data Protection Regulation (GDPR) legislation, it is an offence to post personal information of someone without their permission. People have a right to privacy.

The Prohibition to Incitement of Hatred Act 1989

It is an offence to communicate threatening, abusive or insulting material that is intended or likely to 'stir up' hatred against a group of people because of their race, colour, nationality, religion, ethnic or national origins, membership of the Travelling Community or sexual orientation.

The Three Golden Rules

1. The Granny Rule

Don't post anything you wouldn't want your granny to see.

2. The T-Shirt Rule

Don't post or text anything that you wouldn't put on a t-shirt and walk around wearing all day.

3. The Face Rule

Don't post anything online what you wouldn't say to a person's face in real life.

REFLECTION ON MY LEARNING

Three important things I have learned about sharing information online are:

1. _____

2. _____

3. _____

As a result of what I have learned in this lesson, I will:

_____

_____

_____

RELATIONSHIPS AND SEXUALITY

	Learning Outcomes	Page No.

Relationships and Sexuality

LESSON 16

Learning Outcomes: 1.7, 3.6

By the end of this lesson, you will:

→ understand the broad meaning of sexuality

→ appreciate what a safe, respectful RSE class looks like

→ reflect on what you would like to learn about in RSE class.

KEYWORDS

Sexuality

Sexual activity

Limits of confidentiality

ADDITIONAL RESOURCES

www.belongto.org BeLonG To Youth Service is the national youth service for lesbian, gay, bisexual and transgender young people aged between 14 and 23. There are youth services located in most areas around the country. **Phone: 01 670 6223.**

When students hear they will be looking at relationships and sexuality in class, they often think of it as 'The Talk' or 'Sex Ed', but learning in relationships and sexuality education (or RSE) is much broader than just biological facts. You learn about relationships, how to form healthy and respectful relationships in your life, with friends, family and romantic partners, how to set boundaries in relationships and show respect for the boundaries of others. You will also learn how to take care of your reproductive health and discuss responsible decision-making in relationships and some of the pressures young people experience in relationships.

Revisiting Ground Rules

Ground rules are very important to ensure everyone feels comfortable participating in RSE class. We are now going to recap on the ground rules we visited previously and decide which ground rules will ensure the RSE class is a place where everyone feels happy, safe and respected.

CLASS DISCUSSION

1   Why is it important to have ground rules in RSE class?

2   Do you think there are some ground rules that are particularly important for an RSE class?

3   What are the different ground rules we have already decided on?

4   In RSE class, we cover some very sensitive topics. How do you think we can show respect for others when speaking about gender, sexual orientation and body parts?

105

GROUP ACTIVITY

RSE Ground Rules: Diamond 9

Scattered around the Diamond 9 are different ground rules that would make your RSE class safe and comfortable for everyone. In your small group, discuss each one and decide which rules you think are least important and most important in RSE class. You can add a ground rule your group thinks is important. Then write the ground rules into the Diamond 9.

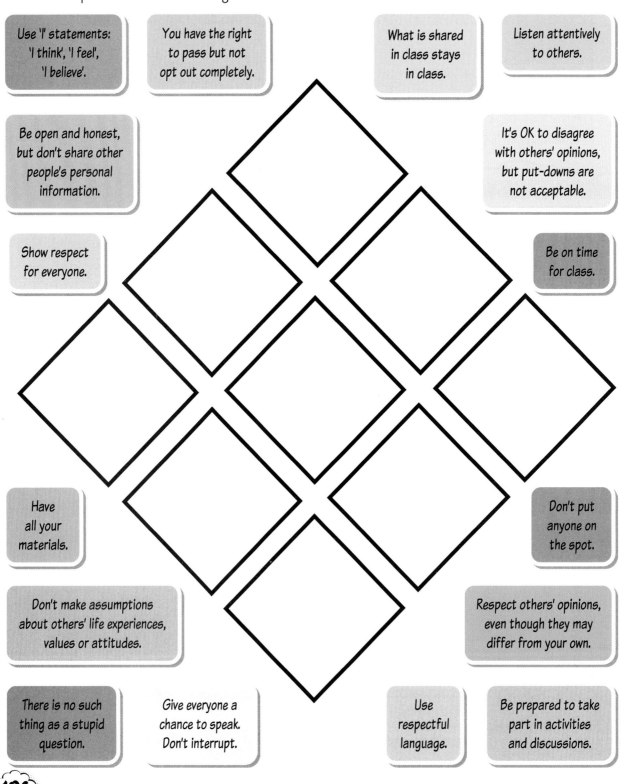

Use 'I' statements: 'I think', 'I feel', 'I believe'.

You have the right to pass but not opt out completely.

What is shared in class stays in class.

Listen attentively to others.

Be open and honest, but don't share other people's personal information.

It's OK to disagree with others' opinions, but put-downs are not acceptable.

Show respect for everyone.

Be on time for class.

Have all your materials.

Don't put anyone on the spot.

Don't make assumptions about others' life experiences, values or attitudes.

Respect others' opinions, even though they may differ from your own.

There is no such thing as a stupid question.

Give everyone a chance to speak. Don't interrupt.

Use respectful language.

Be prepared to take part in activities and discussions.

CLASS ACTIVITY

Choose a reporter from your group to share your group's ground rules with the rest of the class. The whole class must now agree on a set of ground rules. Ensure each ground rule begins with an 'I' statement, e.g. 'I will listen when others are speaking.' When agreement has been reached on these ground rules, write them into the contract. Everyone must sign their own contract to show that they agree.

CLASS CONTRACT

 Signed:

Sexuality

Sexuality – now what does this mean? This can be a very confusing word (even for adults) and it is often confused with sexual orientation, but they are not the same.

> **Sexual orientation** is about who we are emotionally, physically and romantically attracted to. It is just one part of our sexuality.

Sexuality is about our individuality and who we are as a person. There are many different aspects that play a role in forming our sexuality, our personality, the values and beliefs we hold, our relationships, our sexual behaviour, how we interact with others, the image we have of ourselves, the experiences we have, the sex we are assigned at birth, who we are attracted to, what gender we identify as and how we express that gender. Each person has a different idea and understanding of their own sexuality.

The sexuality wheel on the next page helps us to understand the different parts that play a role in forming our sexuality. Each part of the wheel shows one part of who we are and that these parts are all connected and influenced by each other. The boxes on the left side of the wheel show who we are, while the ones on the right show who we are taught or learn to be. These messages may be from family, friends, school, media, religion, our community or culture. Scattered around the wheel are explanations of the different parts that play a role in forming our sexuality. Match each part with its explanation.

Remember!

Limits of confidentiality: There are some things that, if you tell your teacher, they cannot legally keep to themselves. If you tell your teacher or they are made aware that you or any other person is in danger or at risk of being hurt or abused in any way, or if you inform them of a crime or sexual activity, they will have to go further and seek advice from the Designated Liaison Person.

Disclosing personal information: It is important to keep in mind your own privacy and the privacy of others when disclosing personal information. If something in class comes up that concerns you, let your teacher know after class.

Age of consent: In Ireland, it is against the law to have sexual intercourse if you are under 17. This law applies to all relationships.

Coco's Law: Under the Harassment, Harmful Communications and Related Offences Act, otherwise known as Coco's Law, it is illegal to send, receive or share an explicit (nude) image, video or text of someone else without consent.

GROUP ACTIVITY

_____:
The things you believe in and care about. These guide what you believe is right or wrong, e.g. whether you think it is important to treat people with respect.

_____:
How we learn to interact with others and understand what is expected of us in society, e.g. how men and women may be expected to behave in society. It is about how we make friends and fit in with others.

_____:
Various types of activities such as kissing, sexual touching over clothes, touching under clothes, touching genitalia and sexual intercourse. You have probably heard of kissing, scoring, meeting, and so on.

_____:
The way we connect and interact with others; the words, gestures and body language we use to send messages to someone else.

_____:
The people we are connected to in our lives, e.g. family, friends, classmates, intimate partners.

_____:
The things you go through in life. These can be fun or difficult, and can help you grow and learn and sometimes shape who you are as a person.

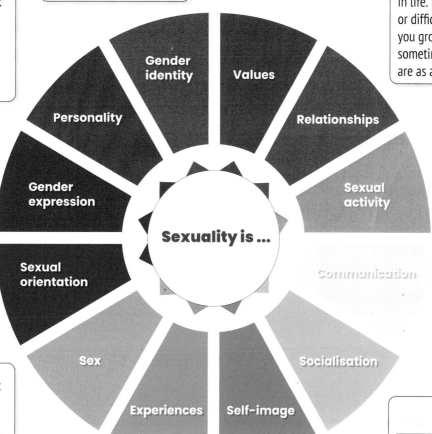

_____:
Our unique qualities and characteristics. It is what sets you apart from others.

_____:
How you see yourself and what you think about yourself. It includes how you feel about your body, what you are good at and how you feel you fit in in the world.

_____:
How we communicate our gender to the outside world, e.g. clothes, hairstyle. It does not always tell us how someone identifies, and we shouldn't assume someone's gender based on their appearance.

_____:
How we think and feel about our own gender. It's a person's deep, internal sense of being male, female, a mixture of both or neither gender.

_____:
This is assigned before or immediately after birth. It is based on the baby's anatomy/external genitalia. The most common sexes assigned at birth are male or female, which generally – but not always – reflect internal hormonal and chromosomal make-up.

_____:
Who we are physically, sexually and romantically attracted to.

109

The Messages We Receive

Growing up can be very exciting – forming new friendships, developing independence and getting to know yourself – but it can also be a very confusing time. We often receive mixed messages about relationships and sexuality. These messages can come from friends, family, media, our culture, religion or other sources. Who do we listen to? What's true and what's not?

Mixed Messages

Look at each of the aspects of sexuality in the table below. In the first column, write down one message we may receive about them from the world around us (e.g. from friends, family, school, media, religion, community or culture). In the second column, write down one impact – positive or negative – that this message might have on young people.

	Message we receive	Impact it might have
Sexual orientation		
Gender expression		
Gender roles		
Body image		
Relationships		
Sexual activity		
Values and beliefs		

REFLECTION ON MY LEARNING

On a blank sheet of paper, complete the statements below about relationships and sexuality. You can do this at home or in another safe space. Drop your sheet into the suggestion box provided by your teacher in the next SPHE class. Don't worry – what you write is completely anonymous. This activity helps you to have a voice in your learning and helps the teacher be more aware of your expectations for RSE class.

I'm interested to know about

I would like to learn more about

I would be uncomfortable talking about

I can go and ask a question to discuss elements that are not clear for me with

LESSON 17
Changes at Adolescence

Learning Outcomes: 1.1, 3.5

connected   resilient   responsible

By the end of this lesson, you will:

•• understand what puberty is and why it happens

•• identify the physical, social and emotional changes that occur during adolescence

•• dispel any inaccurate messages you have received about puberty.

KEYWORDS

Puberty

Adolescence

Emotional

Social

Physical

ADDITIONAL RESOURCES

www.kidshealth.org Provides information on a wide range of topics related to puberty and growing up.

www.childline.ie A 24-hour helpline and online service offering information and support for young people and teenagers. **Freephone 1800 666 666.**

www.barnardos.ie Provides useful advice on a wide range of issues affecting young people.

Changes at Adolescence: Puberty

Puberty is the period of growth the human body goes through when it is changing from a child to an adult. These changes occur to allow people to reproduce and have children one day, if they would like to. **Adolescence** is the time period when puberty occurs.

Puberty starts sometime between the ages of 8 and 14 for girls, and between 9 and 15 for boys. Most typically, people with female-typical anatomy generally begin puberty at 11 years of age and those with male-typical anatomy begin at 12 years of age.

Puberty happens for lots of people regardless of their assigned sex or gender. Everyone goes through puberty at different times and rates. No two people are the same, and some people will start earlier or later than others. These changes are subtle for some people and more dramatic or obvious for others.

PAIR ACTIVITY

Below is a list of changes and challenges that teenagers may experience during puberty. People with male-typical and female-typical anatomies experience similar and different changes.

In pairs, write the number of each change written on the wall into the correct space in the Venn diagram. For example, if you think a change only applies to males, write it into the male side. If you think it only applies to females, write it into the female side. If you think the change applies to both males and females, write it into the intersection.

Go to YouTube and search for 'The Physical Changes That Happen to Most Girls and Boys | Amazing Me' (4:40) to watch a video that will help you understand the physical changes that occur during puberty.

1. Oily skin   2. Growth spurts   3. Mood swings   4. ACNE

5. Conflicting thoughts   6. Wanting to fit in   7. Wet dreams   8. Erections

9. Peer pressure   10. Voice deepens   11. Arguments with parents/guardians   12. Breasts develop

13. Spending more time with peers and friends   14. Shoulders widen   15. Facial hair   16. Want more independence

17. Interest in boys or girls   18. Strong feelings and emotions   19. Getting sexual feelings   20. Greasy hair

21. Feeling lonely and confused   22. Feeling frustrated   23. Underarm hair   24. Concern about appearance

25. Pubic hair   26. Increased sweating   27. Penis growth   28. Increased weight   29. Hips get wider

30. Menstruation begins   31. Eggs are produced   32. Sperm is produced   33. Discharge

34. Nipples get larger   35. Increase in muscle growth   36. Growing pains   37. Sensitive genitals

MALE-TYPICAL CHANGES   BOTH   FEMALE-TYPICAL CHANGES

Social and Emotional Changes

The changes that occur at adolescence are not just physical. As we go through the teenage years our brains are growing and developing too. These changes are referred to as social and emotional changes.

Social changes

These relate to changes in the way you interact with others and how you see yourself. You are seeking more independence and examining where you fit in. You may ask yourself: 'Who am I?', 'Where do I fit in?', 'Am I lovable?'

Emotional changes

These relate to changes in mood and feelings. They occur because our brains are teaching us how to express our feelings and emotions in a grown up-way. We may feel intense emotions at times. This is sometimes referred to as a 'rollercoaster' of emotions.

▶ Go to YouTube and search 'Emotional and Social Changes During Puberty | Amazing Me' (3:00) to help you understand the changes you experience during puberty.

Puberty and Hormones

Puberty begins when a gland in the brain called the pituitary gland sends a message to the brain to release special chemicals called hormones. These hormones trigger the start of the changes that occur during puberty.

In Boys

In boys, hormones travel through the bloodstream and signal the testes to produce testosterone and sperm. Testosterone causes most of the changes in the male body during puberty. It is responsible for muscle development, bone mass and body and facial hair. Sperm cells enable the male to reproduce – to create a baby.

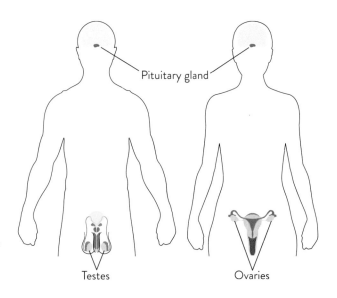

Pituitary gland

Testes

Ovaries

In Girls

In girls, hormones travel through the bloodstream and signal the ovaries to produce oestrogen and progesterone. Oestrogen controls puberty and the menstrual cycle. It is also responsible for the development of breasts and body hair. Progesterone prepares the female body for pregnancy, should it occur.

Looking After Myself During Puberty

It is little wonder with all those hormones zinging around in our bodies that puberty can be a confusing – and sometimes challenging – time for teenagers. During puberty, everyone should feel supported, understood and cared for. Here are some tips for looking after your health and wellbeing during puberty.

Talk to someone you trust

Do not be afraid to reach out and speak to a trusted adult about how you are feeling. Speaking to your friends can also help, as they are going through the same things.

Take time out

If you are having a bad day, experiencing mood swings or feeling overwhelmed, take time out and spend some time alone.

Practise self-love

This can be a difficult time, so try not to be hard on yourself. Practise positive self-talk and show yourself kindness.

Share your feelings

Find a way to express how you are feeling. Keeping a diary, writing poetry or playing music can help you understand and regulate your emotions.

Eat healthy

Eating a healthy balanced diet supports a healthy body and a healthy mind.

Sleep well

Teenagers should get eight to nine hours of sleep every night to be healthy and alert.

Physical activity

Physical activity is great for the mind and body, as it releases hormones that help us feel good. Keep moving!

Look after personal hygiene

Due to all the different changes in our bodies during puberty, we need to pay special attention to our personal hygiene.

> Go to YouTube and search for 'Taking Care of Your Body During Puberty' (2:45) by AMAZE Org for tips about how to keep yourself healthy and clean during puberty.

GROUP ACTIVITY

Commonly Asked Questions During Puberty

During adolescence, we can receive mixed messages about puberty. These messages can come from friends, family and the media. Some of this information is unhelpful and can leave us feeling confused.

The following activity helps to answer some commonly asked questions and rule out misinformation or taboos you may have heard.

Are periods painful?

When will I get my period?

What is a wet dream?

How do I control when I get an erection?

Look at the scenarios on the sticky notes. Use what you have learned in today's lesson to give each person advice on their situation.

I haven't got my period yet and I'm worried in case I get it at school. What should I do?

My friend keeps putting me in awkward situations, pushing me into kissing a girl. I am not comfortable with this. What should I do?

I really like a girl in my class, but I don't know if she likes me. What should I do?

My feelings are all over the place – sometimes I am happy and sometimes I find myself getting wound up, angry and frustrated. I find myself arguing with my parents more. What should I do?

My friend has BO. I heard other people in the class talking about it. What should I do?

I have noticed I am getting a lot more spots. What can I do?

REFLECTION ON MY LEARNING

One way I can support myself during puberty is _____

_____

Someone I could ask for help if I'm worried about anything is _____

_____

A question I am left with from this lesson is _____

_____

LESSON 18
The Reproductive Systems and Reproduction

Learning Outcomes: 1.1, 3.5

responsible   aware

By the end of this lesson, you will:

→ understand the different parts of the male and female reproductive systems and their functions

→ describe what is meant by the menstrual cycle and its role in reproduction

→ appreciate how the physical changes in puberty affect reproduction.

KEYWORDS

Reproductive system
Reproduction
Menstrual cycle

The changes that occur in puberty make it possible for people to have children later in life if they want to. The process of making a baby is called reproduction. In this lesson, you will learn about how reproduction occurs and the different ways people can have children if they want to. We will first examine the reproductive organs.

Reproductive Systems

INDIVIDUAL ACTIVITY

Female Reproductive System

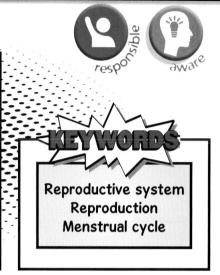

Look at the diagram of the female reproductive system. Match each part with its correct description by writing the correct number in the box beside the description.

Part of reproductive system	Number
Ovaries: Organs where eggs/ova are produced, one on either side of the uterus.	
Uterus (womb): Where the foetus grows during pregnancy. A hollow, pear-shaped organ with a hollow wall. Lining (endometrium) released from the body during menstruation.	
Fallopian tubes: Join uterus to ovaries. During ovulation, egg is released into these.	
Cervix: Lower part of uterus/neck of womb that opens into vagina. During childbirth, can expand about 10cm to allow baby to travel from uterus through vagina and out of mother's body.	
Vagina: Hollow muscular tube connecting uterus to outside of body. Entrance to vagina is outside the body.	
Ovum: Also known as egg. Reproductive cell stored in the ovaries.	

INDIVIDUAL ACTIVITY

Male Reproductive System

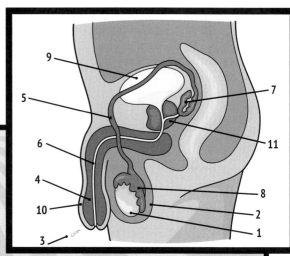

Look at the diagram of the male reproductive system. Match each part with its correct description by writing the correct number in the box beside the description.

Part of reproductive system	Number
Bladder: Muscular sac that stores urine until released from urethra.	
Prostate gland: Walnut-sized gland surrounding portion of the urethra. Produces some of the fluid in semen.	
Vas deferens: Thin, muscular tube that carries sperm to urethra.	
Urethra: Tube that carries urine and semen outside of penis. Urine and semen cannot leave at the same time. When penis is ready to release semen, a valve blocks off bladder so urine cannot leave.	
Foreskin: Loose skin that covers shaft and glans of penis. Can be pulled back gently, allowing penis to be washed and kept clean. Some males have foreskin removed (circumcision). Circumcision does not affect function of penis.	
Scrotum: Sac holding testicles that keeps them at proper temperature to produce healthy sperm (male reproductive cell).	
Seminal vessels: Two small pouches found at base of bladder. Produce thick fluid that helps nourish and carry sperm.	
Sperm: The male reproductive cell.	
Testicles: Two egg-shaped glands that produce sperm.	
Epididymis: Tube at back of each testicle that joins urethra.	
Penis: Made of two parts: shaft (main part) and glans (tip, sometimes called the 'head'). Penis delivers sperm and urine through urethra. Made of spongy tissue. Sometimes the spongy tissue fills with blood and becomes hard (erection). This usually happens when a person is sexually aroused but can happen unexpectedly during puberty. (Wet dream: Where a person gets an erection and sperm-containing semen is ejaculated while sleeping.)	

Not everyone's genitals look the same or resemble what is shown in the diagram. Variations in size and shape are normal and healthy.

INDIVIDUAL ACTIVITY

Fill in the blanks below with words you learned and remember about the reproductive systems from the previous activity.

1. The Journey of the Egg

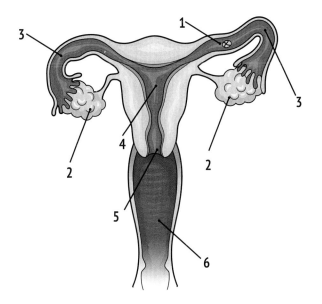

Word bank

uterus
menstrual cycle
vagina
ovary
egg
cervix
fallopian tube
menstruation
period

Each month, an **1.** _____ matures and is released from an
2. _____ . Typically, the two ovaries alternate releasing eggs — one month the left ovary releases an egg, the next month the right ovary does. This process is called ovulation.

The egg travels along the **3.** _____ _____ . In the days before ovulation, a thick, soft lining made up of tissue and blood builds up along the walls of the **4.** _____ . This lining contains nutrients to nourish a growing foetus if the egg is fertilised and pregnancy occurs. If the egg is not fertilised, it does not attach to the wall of the uterus. The brain sends a message to the uterus lining that it is not needed any more. When this happens, the uterus sheds its lining and it passes through the **5.** _____ into the **6.** _____ and out of the body. This is called **7.** _____ , more commonly known as a **8.** _____ . It usually lasts between two and seven days.

As soon as the period occurs, hormones invite a new lining to grow. The whole process is called the **9.** _____ _____ .

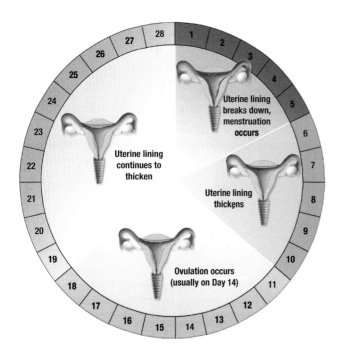

Uterine lining breaks down, menstruation occurs

Uterine lining thickens

Ovulation occurs (usually on Day 14)

Uterine lining continues to thicken

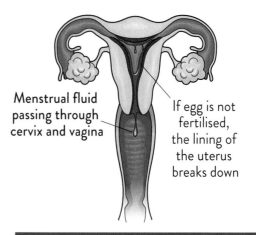

Menstrual fluid passing through cervix and vagina

If egg is not fertilised, the lining of the uterus breaks down

AGE OF CONSENT
In Ireland, it is illegal to have sex with anyone under the age of 17.

2. The Journey of the Sperm

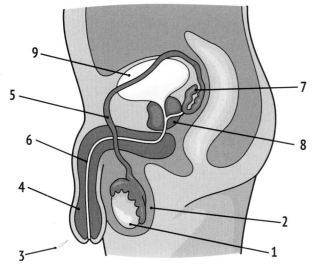

Word bank

urethra

scrotum

penis

testicles

bladder

sperm

seminal vesicles

prostate gland

vas deferens

The **1.** _____, which are held in a sac called the **2.** _____, produce the reproductive cell called **3.** _____. During sexual intercourse or sexual arousal, these sperm are released from the testicles.

First, the **4.** _____ gets larger and firmer and sticks out from the body. This is called an erection. When released the sperm travel up a long thin tube called the

5. _____ _____ all the way to the **6.** _____. Along the way, sperm mixes with fluids from the **7.** _____

_____ and the **8.** _____ _____. This fluid called semen helps the sperm to swim. When the penis is ready to release semen, a valve blocks off the **9.** _____ so urine cannot escape. When the sperm leaves the penis, this is called ejaculation. After this, the erection goes away and the penis gets smaller.

Reproduction

Fertilisation

During sex, the erect penis is inserted into the vagina. Sperm are ejaculated into the vagina and swim up past the cervix, through the uterus and into the fallopian tubes. If the sperm meets an egg in the fallopian tube, each sperm cell will attempt to penetrate the egg. Only one sperm will succeed in penetrating the egg, which is called fertilisation. Once one sperm has penetrated the egg, the outer membrane of the egg hardens and prevents fertilisation by any other sperm.

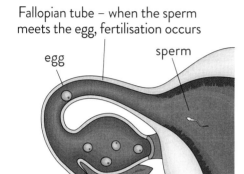

Fallopian tube – when the sperm meets the egg, fertilisation occurs

egg

sperm

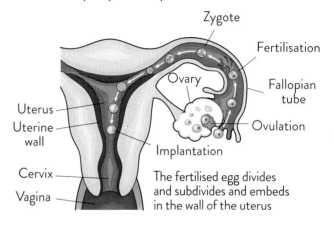

Zygote

Fertilisation

Ovary

Fallopian tube

Uterus

Uterine wall

Ovulation

Implantation

Cervix

Vagina

The fertilised egg divides and subdivides and embeds in the wall of the uterus

Implantation

After fertilisation the fertilised egg forms a cell called a zygote which begins to divide and subdivide. The zygote travels down the rest of the fallopian tube and into the uterus. About 5–7 days after fertilisation, the zygote divides into an embryo and a placenta and embeds itself in the lining of the uterus. This is called implantation.

Some Interesting Facts

- Sperm can live for up to seven days from the time of ejaculation.
- Only one sperm can penetrate an egg. As soon as the egg has been penetrated, a barrier forms to prevent another sperm from entering.
- An egg is about the size of a full stop.
- Someone with female-typical anatomy is born with approximately 1 million immature eggs in their ovaries.
- An egg must be fertilised by a sperm within 48 hours of its release from the ovary.
- Eggs are pushed along the fallopian tubes by the movement of tiny hairs.
- The menstruation cycle of a teenager can be irregular until the body adapts. Stress, illness and changes in diet or routine can all affect the menstrual cycle.
- The first period is called the menarche.
- Approximately 200–500 million sperm cells can be released during each ejaculation.
- Non-identical (fraternal) twins happen when two eggs are released at the same time and are fertilised by two different sperm.
- Identical twins happen when one fertilised egg splits and develops two foetuses with exactly the same genetic information.

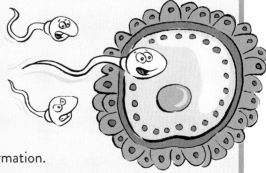

INDIVIDUAL ACTIVITY

Reproduction Crossword

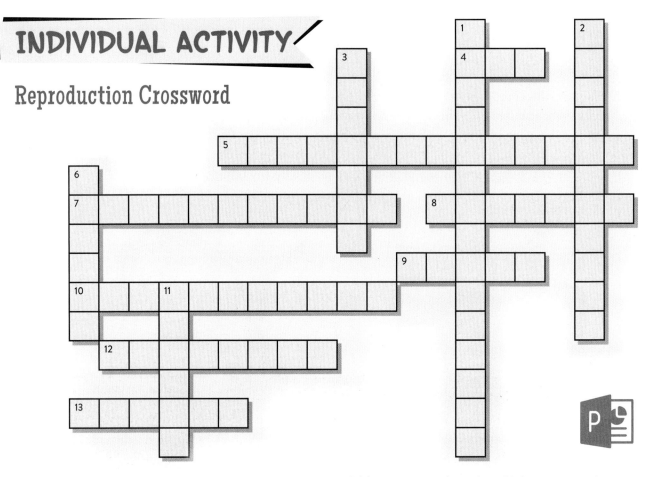

Across

4 The female reproductive cell.

5 Thin tubes that connect the ovaries to the uterus.

7 Another name for the lining of the womb.

8 A muscular bag that holds urine.

9 The male reproductive cell.

10 The release of sperm from the erect penis.

12 Sometimes removed from the tip of the male penis, but it does not affect its function.

13 Narrow muscular tube which connects the uterus to the outside of the body.

Down

1 These produce a fluid which helps to carry sperm.

2 A thin tube carrying semen to the urethra.

3 External sac that holds and keeps the testicles at the proper temperature.

6 These produce sperm.

11 Neck of the womb through which the baby passes during childbirth.

REFLECTION ON MY LEARNING

Something I learned in this lesson that I didn't know before was _____

_____

_____

A question I still have is _____

_____

LESSON 19

Gender Stereotypes

Learning Outcomes: 1.5, 1.6

 connected respected responsible

By the end of this lesson, you will:

↠ explore examples of gender stereotyping

↠ reflect on how gender stereotypes can affect behaviours, attitudes and relationships

↠ recognise and identify gender stereotypes in the media.

KEYWORDS

Gender stereotypes

ADDITIONAL RESOURCES

www.belongto.org BeLonG To Youth Service is the national youth service for lesbian, gay, bisexual and transgender young people aged between 14 and 23. There are youth services located in most areas around the country.

CLASS ACTIVITY

Your teacher will read out the following words. For each word, put one hand up if you think it's a 'girl thing', put both hands up if you think it's a 'boy thing', or keep your hands down if you think it could be a 'both' thing.

- handbag
- trucks
- shirt
- engineer
- pilot
- nurse
- motorbike
- home economics
- caregiver
- leggings
- make-up
- flowers
- trousers
- blue
- work overalls
- drummer
- dance
- woodwork
- wine
- highlights
- nail varnish
- bikini
- beautician
- apron
- strong
- pink
- surgeon
- shopping
- hair extensions
- ponytail
- dolls
- skirt
- glitter
- cars
- muscular
- weights
- gossip
- plumber
- eyelashes
- sensitive

CLASS DISCUSSION

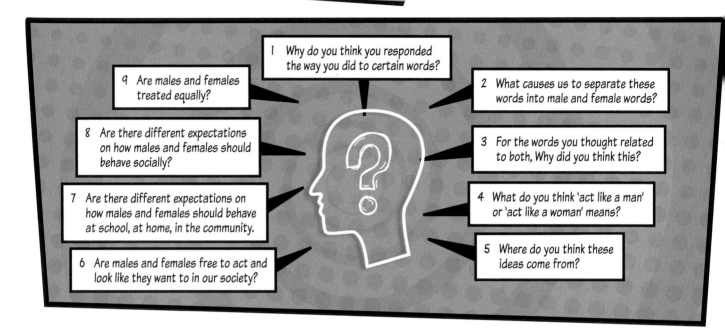

1 Why do you think you responded the way you did to certain words?

9 Are males and females treated equally?

2 What causes us to separate these words into male and female words?

8 Are there different expectations on how males and females should behave socially?

3 For the words you thought related to both, Why did you think this?

7 Are there different expectations on how males and females should behave at school, at home, in the community.

4 What do you think 'act like a man' or 'act like a woman' means?

6 Are males and females free to act and look like they want to in our society?

5 Where do you think these ideas come from?

Gender Stereotyping

Gender stereotyping means having certain expectations of people because they happen to be male or female. The belief that people should act or look a certain way because of their gender. These gender stereotypes affect so many aspects of our lives from our appearance to how we act to the hobbies we have and the careers we pursue. They can limit who we can be, what we can do and the choices we make.

Types of Gender Stereotypes	Examples
Personality: Assuming men and women should have certain personality traits	'Boys don't show their emotions'
Domestic behaviour: Assuming men and women have certain roles in the family	'Women are caregivers'
Occupation: Assuming men are suited better to certain occupations and women to others	'Men are better suited to manual labour'
Physical appearance: Assuming men and women should look, dress or act in a certain way	'Boys shouldn't wear nail varnish'

Gender norms and stereotyping are ingrained in us from a young age. Baby girls are often dressed in pink, and baby boys in blue. Toys are often gifted based on gender: the pretty baby doll for the girl and the toy toolbox for the boy.

We assign gender to lots of different things – clothes, hairstyles, behaviour, hobbies and careers. This stereotyping continues throughout childhood into adolescence and then adulthood. It is unrealistic and unfair to expect people to look or behave a certain way based on their genitals.

PAIR ACTIVITY

In pairs, write some common male and female stereotypes in and around each figure.

GROUP ACTIVITY

In your small groups, answer the following questions. Give feedback to your class.

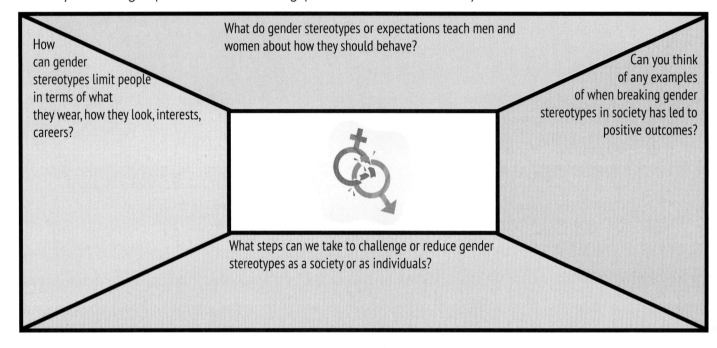

How can gender stereotypes limit people in terms of what they wear, how they look, interests, careers?

What do gender stereotypes or expectations teach men and women about how they should behave?

Can you think of any examples of when breaking gender stereotypes in society has led to positive outcomes?

What steps can we take to challenge or reduce gender stereotypes as a society or as individuals?

Gender Stereotyping and the Media

Gender stereotypes can be so fixed in our minds that sometimes we don't question them. Our culture bombards us with messages about what it means to be male or female. It can be easy to see how family, friends and classmates influence gender stereotypes, but it may not be as easy to identify how the media influences us. The messages we receive from advertisements and the media can influence how we think and feel and can reinforce gender stereotypes.

Look at the images below and discuss the questions that follow as a class.

CLASS DISCUSSION

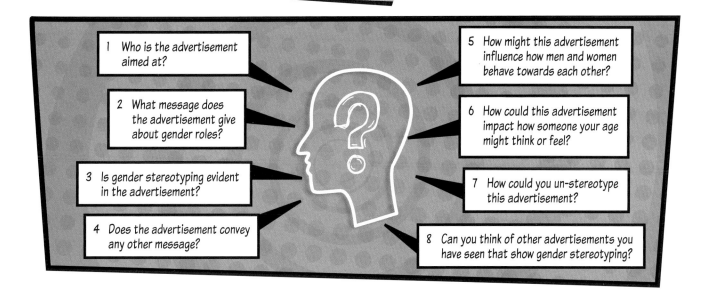

1 Who is the advertisement aimed at?

2 What message does the advertisement give about gender roles?

3 Is gender stereotyping evident in the advertisement?

4 Does the advertisement convey any other message?

5 How might this advertisement influence how men and women behave towards each other?

6 How could this advertisement impact how someone your age might think or feel?

7 How could you un-stereotype this advertisement?

8 Can you think of other advertisements you have seen that show gender stereotyping?

REFLECTION ON MY LEARNING

Discuss the following prompt with the person next to you for one minute.

Something I can do to reduce gender stereotyping is

_____

_____

_____

_____

_____

LESSON 20

Gender and Gender Identity

Learning Outcomes: 1.4, 1.5, 1.6, 1.7, 3.6

 responsible connected aware

By the end of this lesson, you will:

→ understand various terms related to gender identity

→ understand how gender identity is experienced and expressed

→ understand the difference between gender identity and sexual orientation

→ recognise the importance of respecting all genders.

KEYWORDS

Gender
Sex assigned at birth
Gender expression
Sexual orientation
Pronouns

ADDITIONAL RESOURCES

www.belongto.org BeLonG To Youth Service is the national youth service for lesbian, gay, bisexual and transgender young people aged between 14 and 23. There are youth services located in most areas around the country.

The Genderbread Person

You have probably heard the words gender, gender identity, sex, sexual orientation. These words can be confusing, even for adults. The Genderbread Person can help us to understand the different components of gender by explaining the terms 'gender identity', 'gender expression' and 'sex assigned at birth'. It also helps us to understand the difference between sexual orientation and gender identity.

THE GENDERBREAD PERSON

Gender expression: How we communicate our gender to the outside world, e.g. clothes, hairstyle, name. Gender expression does not always tell us how someone identifies their gender, and we should not assume how someone feels on the inside.

Gender identity: How we think and feel about our own gender. It's a deep, internal sense of being male, female, a mixture of both or none at all.

Sex: Assigned before or immediately after birth, sex is based on the baby's anatomy/external genitalia. The most common sexes assigned at birth are male or female. These generally – but not always – reflect the baby's internal hormonal and chromosomal make-up.

Sexual orientation: Who we are attracted to emotionally, physically and sexually.

CLASS ACTIVITY

 Go to YouTube and search for 'Range of Gender Identities' (2:56) by AMAZE Org to learn more about gender identity. After watching the video, discuss the questions below with your classmates.

CLASS DISCUSSION

1 What is the main message you received from watching this clip?

2 Do you think society places expectations on males and females on how they should act, feel and behave?

3 Where do you think we learn these roles?

4 Do you think different cultures have different expectations for appropriate ways for males and females to behave?

5 How would these expectations affect how males and females behave in their daily lives?

6 Have you ever felt you were treated differently because of your sex assigned at birth?

7 How can we show respect for all genders?

INDIVIDUAL ACTIVITY

Gender Identity Words and Pronouns

 Go to YouTube and search for 'Gender Identity and Pronouns – What Will You Teach The World?' (3:42) to learn more about the different ways that people identify. After watching the video, complete the activity below by matching the terms to their definitions.

| Gender expression | Misgendering | Non-binary | Cisgender |
| Transgender | Gender identity | Pronouns | Sex assigned at birth |

This is based on a baby's anatomy/ external genitalia.

A person whose gender matches the sex they were assigned at birth.

When someone uses the wrong pronoun to describe someone else.

Words we use to refer to someone instead of their name. They usually reflect the gender of the person being spoken about.

How we show our gender to the world through clothing, hairstyles, etc.

A person whose gender identity does not match their assigned sex at birth.

A deep personal sense of one's own gender: male, female, both or neither.

A person who feels they are not simply masculine or feminine, but a mix of genders.

GROUP ACTIVITY

Respecting Difference

 Go to YouTube and search for 'What Is Transgender?' (1:14) by BeLonG To Youth Services. Watch the video, then search for 'Name and Pronoun' (1:23), also by BeLonG To Youth Services. Once you have watched both videos, use what you learned from today's lesson to create a guide to showing respect for all genders.

GUIDE FOR RESPECTING GENDER IDENTITY

REFLECTION ON MY LEARNING

Three things I learned in this lesson were:

1. _____

2. _____

3. _____

As a result of this lesson, I will

_____

_____

LESSON 21

Sexual Orientation

Learning Outcomes: 1.4, 3.6, 4.7, 4.8

respected   connected   resilient   responsible

By the end of this lesson, you will:

→ have explored what sexual orientation means

→ have a greater understanding of the language used in relation to sexual orientation

→ appreciate that sexual orientation is expressed and experienced in different ways

→ reflect on the experiences of being an LGBTQ+ young person

→ have discussed the issues arising for LGBTQ+ young people

→ have explored ways of showing support for LGBTQ+ young people.

KEYWORDS

Sexual orientation

LGBTQ+

Ally

ADDITIONAL RESOURCES

www.lgbt.ie A support and education organisation that works to help and enhance the lives of LGBTQ+ people in Ireland. **Phone 1890929539.**

www.belongto.org Offers support and advice for lesbian, gay, bisexual and transgender young people.

In previous lessons, you explored gender and gender identity, and learned that gender identity and sexual orientation are not the same thing.

Gender identity: How we think and feel about our own gender. It's a deep, internal sense of being male, female, a mixture of both or none at all.

Sexual orientation: Who we are attracted to emotionally, physically and sexually.

Go to YouTube and search for 'Sexual Orientations Explained: Lesbian, Gay, Heterosexual and Bisexual' (2:02) to help you understand what sexual orientation is.

LGBTQ+ is an umbrella term that represents a range of different sexual orientations and gender identities.

L = Lesbian

G = Gay

B = Bisexual

T = Transgender

Q = Queer

+ all other minority sexual orientations and gender identities

In this lesson, we will look at sexual orientation. We will look at what it means, how it is expressed and how to use respectful, inclusive language in relation to it, as well as how we can support all LGBTQ+ people in our lives.

 Go to YouTube and search for 'What Is Heteronormativity? ft. Beckii Cruel & Calum McSwiggan | Voice Box | Childline' (4:43).

LOVE IS LOVE

LOVE IS LOVE

LOVE IS LOVE

LOVE IS LOVE

INDIVIDUAL ACTIVITY

Inclusive Language Crossword

There are a lot of words that are related to sexual orientation, and some can be a little confusing. Complete the crossword below to help familiarise yourself with the different words and their meaning.

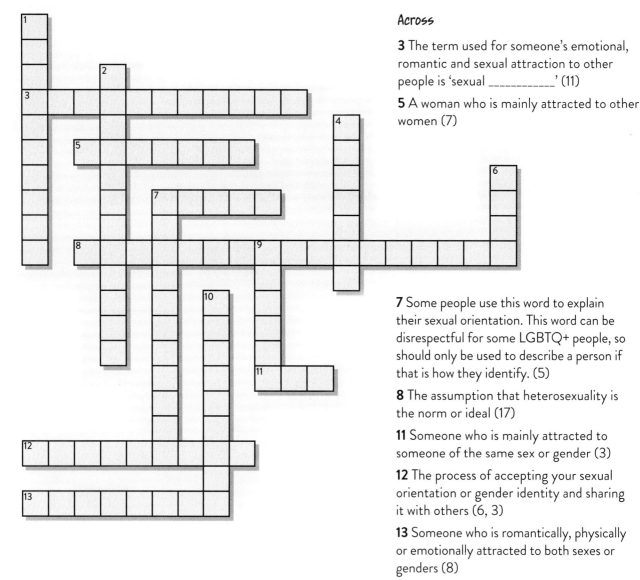

Across

3 The term used for someone's emotional, romantic and sexual attraction to other people is 'sexual _____' (11)

5 A woman who is mainly attracted to other women (7)

7 Some people use this word to explain their sexual orientation. This word can be disrespectful for some LGBTQ+ people, so should only be used to describe a person if that is how they identify. (5)

8 The assumption that heterosexuality is the norm or ideal (17)

11 Someone who is mainly attracted to someone of the same sex or gender (3)

12 The process of accepting your sexual orientation or gender identity and sharing it with others (6, 3)

13 Someone who is romantically, physically or emotionally attracted to both sexes or genders (8)

Down

1 Negative feelings, attitudes or beliefs directed at gay people, or those perceived to be lesbian or gay (10)

2 Someone who is attracted to someone whose sex or gender is different to their own (12)

4 Someone who is not necessarily sexually attracted to others, but may feel romantic or emotional attraction (7)

6 Anyone who supports the LGBTQ+ community, regardless of their own sexual orientation or gender identity, and takes a stand against bullying and harassment (4)

7 The process of exploring your sexual orientation, gender identity or gender expression (11)

9 The deliberate or accidental sharing of another person's sexual orientation or gender identity (6)

10 Someone who may be attracted to any person, regardless of their sex assigned at birth or gender identity (9)

134

Being LGBTQ+ in Ireland Today

In recent years, we have seen lots of positive changes in relation to the rights and community support for LGBTQ+ people. We have seen the legalisation of same-sex marriage in 2015 and greater representation of LGBTQ+ people in the media.

Thankfully, today's society is a more open place than it was in the past, and in general people feel more confident about coming out and celebrating their sexual orientation and gender identity. This is largely due to the fact they feel they have support from their family and friends, community and neighbourhood.

Although there have been a number of positive changes for the LGBTQ+ community, for LGBTQ+ young people, accepting your sexual orientation and/or gender identity can still bring feelings of fear and isolation. Lesbian, gay, bisexual and transgender students are part of every student body, yet some LGBTQ+ young people report having negative experiences at school.

Below are the key findings of the School Climate Survey, a study that reports the lived experiences of LGBTQ+ teenagers at schools in the Republic of Ireland today.

- → 76% of LGBTQ+ young people feel unsafe at school.

- → 1 in 3 LGBTQ+ students reported that other students are not accepting of LGBTQ+ identities.

- → 69% of LGBTQ+ students hear homophobic remarks from other students.

- → 1 in 3 LGBTQ+ students have skipped school to avoid negative treatment from other students.

- → LGBTQ+ students have avoided PE class, bathrooms, locker rooms and lunch areas due to feeling unsafe.

- → 41% of LGBTQ+ students experience cyberbullying via social media, phone or email.

- → **99% of LGBTQ+ students knew at least one school staff member supportive of LGBTQ+ identities.**

Did You Know?

- On average, 6–10% of any group of young people may identify as LGBTQ+.

If 6% of people = LGBTQ+

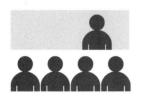   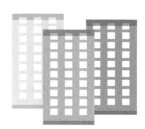

IN A CLASS OF 30	**IN A SCHOOL OF 300**	**IN A VILLAGE OF 3000**	**IN A CITY OF 300,000**
1–2 are LGBTQ+	18 are LGBTQ+	180 are LGBTQ+	18,000 are LGBTQ+

Source: BeLonG To

- The average age for a young person to become aware of their sexual orientation and/or gender identity is 12.
- The average age for coming out is 16.
- The intervening years can be a lonely and isolating time.
- Sexual orientation is not a choice and cannot be changed.
- The Equality Status Act prohibits the harassment of individuals based on their sexual orientation.
- Same-sex marriage has been legal in Ireland since 2015.
- There are many support groups to help LGBTQ+ young people. Ask your teacher or search online if you would like more information.

AGE OF CONSENT

The legal age of consent in Ireland is 17. It is the same for all sexual orientations.

Stand Up Week

Every year across Ireland, Stand Up Awareness Week takes place. This week gives second-level schools, Youthreach and youth services the opportunity to celebrate and recognise the LGBTQ+ community. It also offers an opportunity to take steps to make spaces safe and supportive for LGBTQ+ young people. It is a time when we show solidarity with young people and others, to ensure they feel seen, heard and safe, and to ensure that everyone knows that biphobic, homophobic and transphobic bullying will not be tolerated.

> Findings indicate that LGBTQ+ students were more likely to feel accepted by their peers and had an increased sense of belonging when such support exists.

The Pride Flag

We often see the LGBTQ+ flag flying in town, outside businesses and at people's homes. But what does it actually mean, and what do the colours represent?

Gilbert Baker (1951–2017) was an American artist, gay rights activist and designer of the **rainbow flag** (1978). Baker's flag became widely associated with LGBTQ+ rights and is a symbol of gay pride that can be seen everywhere in the decades since its debut.

Gilbert Baker's flag has a lot of meaning – each colour represents something different.

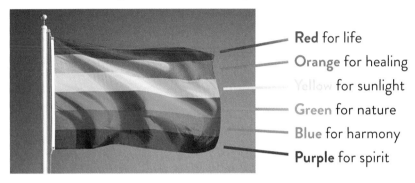

— **Red** for life
— **Orange** for healing
— Yellow for sunlight
— **Green** for nature
— **Blue** for harmony
— **Purple** for spirit

Showing Respect

CLASS ACTIVITY

 Go to YouTube and search for 'Shh! Silence Helps Homophobia - LGBT Youth Scotland'. Watch the first part of the video and press pause at 3:06. Discuss the questions below with your classmates.

1. What do you think the message 'Silence helps homophobia' means?

2. How do you think the boy in the video is feeling in each scene?

3. What do you think of what the bystander does in each scenario?

4. How can the language we use like 'That's so gay' be disrespectful?

5. How could the different people in the video stand up and show support for the young person?

Finish watching the video and discuss the following questions

6. How did you feel after watching the second half of the video? Has it made you think? In what way?

7. Why do you think people engage in homophobic bullying?

8. How can we all play a role in standing up to homophobic bullying and being an ally?

REFLECTION ON MY LEARNING

In pairs, write down five things your school could do to ensure that LGBTQ+ students feel respected and have a positive experience while at school (e.g. in SPHE class, the student council, anti-bullying policy, code of behaviour). Then write down individual behaviours that would help in creating spaces where LGBTQ+ people are safe and supported to be themselves.

Supportive school environment

1. _____

2. _____

3. _____

4. _____

5. _____

Supportive individual behaviour

1. _____

2. _____

3. _____

4. _____

5. _____

 Go to YouTube and search for 'How To Be A LGBTQIA+ Ally' (2:01) by Amaze Org. Does your school have a GSA or LGBTQ+ club? Could you start one?

HELP AND SUPPORT

The **National LGBT Helpline** provides a confidential listening, support and information service to lesbian, gay, bisexual and transgender people. The service is also used by people who are questioning if they might be LGBTQ+, as well as the family and friends of LGBTQ+ people and professionals looking for information. The service is volunteer-run and operates Monday to Friday from 7 p.m. to 9 p.m., Saturday and Sunday 3 p.m. to 6 p.m.

Website: www.lgbt.ie

Email: info@lgbt.ie

Call: 1890 929 539

BeLonG To Youth Service is the national youth service for lesbian, gay, bisexual and transgender young people aged between 14 and 23. There are youth services located in most areas around the country.

Website: www.belongto.org

Email: info@belongto.ie

Call or WhatsApp: 01 670 6223

LESSON 22

Understanding and Setting Healthy Boundaries

Learning Outcomes: 1.2, 1.7, 3.1, 3.2, 3.4

 respected
 connected
 responsible
 aware
 resilient

By the end of this lesson, you will:

- understand the different types of boundaries
- recognise that everyone has different boundaries
- consider how to show respect for other people's boundaries
- appreciate the importance of setting healthy boundaries.

KEYWORDS

Boundaries

Consent

Sexting

ADDITIONAL RESOURCES

www.childline.ie A 24-hour helpline and online service offering information and support for young people and teenagers. **Freephone 1800 666 666.**

www.barnardos.ie Provides useful advice on a wide range of issues affecting young people.

Setting Healthy Boundaries

Boundaries are the personnel rules we set ourselves about how we want to be treated in our relationships and friendships. Having boundaries lets other people know what you are comfortable with and what you are not comfortable with.

Setting healthy boundaries allows you to stay true to yourself and to your values.

Types of Boundaries

Personal boundaries:

These boundaries relate to how you want to be treated by others. Think about how you would or would not like people to speak to you, what and how much information you want to share with others, and how much or little of your time you wish to share with others.

Physical boundaries:

These relate to physical touch and personal space and what a person is comfortable with. The kind of touch you feel comfortable with from a friend, boyfriend, girlfriend, family member, acquaintance or stranger are all different, so it's good to think about how close you want these people to be to you.

139

Identifying My Boundaries and Others' Boundaries

INDIVIDUAL ACTIVITY

Read the 10 statements below. Your teacher will hand out a worksheet containing the same statements. For each statement on the worksheet, put a **tick** for Yes, No or Sometimes, depending on how you feel.

Important: This activity is anonymous, so no one will know how you have answered. Write your answers in pencil, and do not write your name on the top of the worksheet.

1. I am OK with people hugging me.

2. I like people at my feet.

3. I enjoy sharing photos and posts online.

4. I am OK with speaking in class.

5. I don't mind other people posting pictures of me online.

6. I'm OK with sharing my food with others.

7. I like to spend time on my own.

8. I'm OK with sharing personal information with friends.

9. I like to share my homework for others to copy.

10. I don't like when people get too close when they are talking to me.

CLASS ACTIVITY

Your teacher will now collect the sheets. Everyone will receive someone else's answers. As your teacher goes through each statement, you must put a thumbs up for yes, thumbs down for no and thumbs sideways for sometimes. Record the class's total answers for each statement in the sheet below.

Question	Yes 👍	No 👎	Sometimes 👍
1.			
2.			
3.			
4.			
5.			
6.			
7.			
8.			
9.			
10.			

CLASS DISCUSSION

1 What is the main message you received from doing this activity?

2 Why do you think your classmates had different answers?

3 What verbal or non-verbal clues do you think would help us recognise overstepping the boundaries of our friends, classmates or family members?

4 Why do you think it is important to recognise other people's boundaries?

Setting and Respecting Our Boundaries and the Boundaries of Others

Think of boundaries as a line on the ground that we don't want other people to cross. Boundaries will differ from person to person. What one person is comfortable with another may not be.

Everyone has their own physical and personal boundaries. All boundaries are valid. A person's boundaries may also depend on the relationship they have with the other person, e.g. with family, friends, in school or online. We should respect other people's boundaries by not doing or saying anything that would make them feel uncomfortable.

Challenges to Setting Healthy Boundaries

Below are some reasons why it can be difficult to set healthy boundaries. Can you add some others?

Fear of being excluded from a friend group

The need to make other people happy

Fear of the other person's reaction

Worry about what others will think of you

Others will make you feel bad

How to Set Clear Boundaries

Listen to your body

Our bodies can give us the best clues as to whether our boundary has been crossed. Is the situation making you feel uncomfortable, anxious or overwhelmed? Sometimes we just have a gut feeling if something is right or wrong for us.

Communicate your boundary

Be assertive – say exactly what you feel so the other person gets the message. Use 'I' statements, like 'I feel uncomfortable when ...'

Don't let others make you feel bad

You don't have to explain yourself or why you are setting a certain boundary. Only you know what is right or wrong for you.

Set consequences

Let the other person know what will happen if they continue to cross your boundary, e.g. 'If you raise your voice again, I will leave.' If the person continues to cross your boundary, you may need to end this relationship. Be clear and firm, but polite.

Talk to a trusted adult

If anyone makes you feel uncomfortable in any way, you should talk to a trusted adult about it. They can offer you advice about how to handle the situation.

INDIVIDUAL ACTIVITY

What Does Setting Boundaries Sound Like?

Below are some things you can say if others are crossing your boundaries. Add your own to the empty boxes.

I don't feel like talking about this right now.

I am not comfortable with this.

I'm not finding this funny. Please stop.

I need you to listen to me or I'm leaving.

That's not something I'm comfortable sharing.

I can only stay for half an hour.

I need time to think about it. I'll get back to you.

I don't want to.

I've decided not to.

I'm not happy with this.

I'm not sure.

I don't feel ready.

I've changed my mind.

We are moving too fast.

This doesn't feel right.

Go to YouTube and search for 'Setting Healthy Boundaries' (3:38) to watch a video about how to set boundaries.

GROUP ACTIVITY

Your teacher will assign your group one of the scenarios below. Read the scenario and discuss and answer the following questions.

1. What boundary has been crossed?
2. How might the person be feeling?
3. Why might it be difficult for them to communicating how they are feeling?
4. What advice would you give them?

Ciara

Ciara and Joanne have gone to the beach for a day out. Ciara loves the beach, but she is feeling a little self-conscious in her bikini. Joanne decides to take a selfie and encourages Ciara to get in the picture. Joanne is very pleased with the photo and is keen to put it up on Instagram, #beachdaze! Ciara is not happy with the picture and asks Joanne not to post it, as she would feel very uncomfortable with all of Joanne's followers seeing her in her bikini. Joanne tells her 'Don't be ridiculous, you look fab!'

Sam

Sam loves English. The class has been assigned a short story to write for homework. He spends a long time planning and writing his piece. He gets to school the next morning and goes to the canteen to meet his friend, Eoghan. Eoghan explains to Sam that he didn't have time to write the story. He asks for Sam's copy and says that he can just use some of Sam's ideas and write something slightly different. Sam tells Eoghan he is worried in case the teacher spots he copied it. Eoghan assures Sam that the teacher will never notice and that it is no big deal. He tells Sam that he would do the same for him.

Sunisa

Sunisa is in a WhatsApp group with her friends. They chat about everything going on in their lives. Sunisa enjoys the chats and loves keeping up with all of the girls' stories. Lately, however, there seems to be no end to the messages coming through. Michelle always starts conversations really late at night and expects all of the girls to respond. If Sunisa doesn't respond, all of the girls badger her the next day, asking her why she was not engaging with the group chat. She is so tired of staying up late, reading and responding to messages on her phone.

Mia

Mia's aunt has always been very affectionate and kind. She is a very tactile person and loves to greet Mia at the door with a hug when she visits. Mia has never particularly enjoyed being hugged or touched, especially by people she is not very close with. Mia's own parents know this and understand her feelings. Mia feels very uncomfortable when her aunt hugs her like this. She understands that she is just showing affection but would prefer if she did it in another way.

143

Daniel

Daniel really likes a girl he has been chatting with in his Home Economics class, called Shelly. He trusts his friend Chris and tells him about Shelly while they are having lunch in the canteen. Chris tells him that he has to make a move, and kiss her. He tells Daniel that Shelly is really popular, and if he doesn't act quickly, someone else will take their chance. Chris even tells Daniel that he will talk to Shelly. Daniel feels extremely uncomfortable about what Chris is saying to him.

What is Consent?

Consent is when you agree to do something or give your permission for something to happen. We learn about consent from a very young age, asking people for permission to do certain things, listening to others and respecting their answer.

Consent is part of respecting people's physical boundaries and is important for healthy relationships.

> For all sexual activity, whether it be holding hands, kissing, touching or anything else, you need to ask permission or seek consent.

 Go to YouTube and search for 'Consent Explained: What Is It?' (1:47) by AMAZE Org to help you understand consent and sexual activity.

REFLECTION ON MY LEARNING

In each of the fingers below, write down one boundary you would set for yourself:

- with friends
- with family
- online
- in the community
- at school.

EMOTIONAL WELLBEING

LESSON 23 — Emotional Wellbeing

connected resilient aware

Learning Outcomes: 4.1, 4.4

By the end of this lesson, you will:

↠ understand what emotional wellbeing means

↠ appreciate what you can do to look after your emotional wellbeing

↠ recognise that having ups and downs is a normal part of life.

KEYWORDS

Emotional wellbeing
Mindfulness

ADDITIONAL RESOURCES

Text 50808 A free, anonymous 24-hour messaging service that provides everything from a calming chat to immediate support. This text service is a safe space where you are listened to by a trained volunteer. By asking questions, listening to you and responding with support, they will help you sort through your feelings until you both feel you are now in a calm, safe place.

www.ispcc.ie/teenline A national 24-hour helpline service for teenagers up to the age of 18 in Ireland. They can be contacted 24 hours a day, 365 days a year, online or by calling **1800 833 634**.

www.jigsaw.ie Provides information and advice on a range of issues faced by young people.

www.bodywhys.ie Bodywhys is a national charity offering information and support to people affected by eating disorders. **Phone: 01 2107906.**

What is Emotional Wellbeing?

Emotional wellbeing is an important part of our overall health. It is about having the skills to cope with the ups and downs of everyday life. Everyone has good days and bad days. We can't all feel good all the time; our emotional wellbeing changes and this is a normal part of life. We can learn the skills to help us meet any challenges we are confronted with.

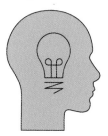

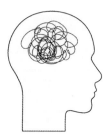
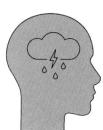

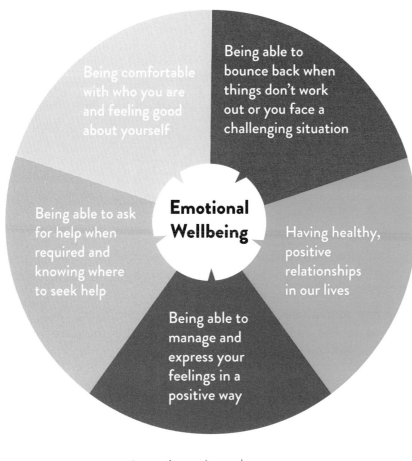

Emotional Wellbeing

- Being comfortable with who you are and feeling good about yourself
- Being able to bounce back when things don't work out or you face a challenging situation
- Having healthy, positive relationships in our lives
- Being able to manage and express your feelings in a positive way
- Being able to ask for help when required and knowing where to seek help

Our Emotional Wellbeing Seesaw

When thinking about our emotional wellbeing, it can be useful to compare it to a seesaw. Like a seesaw, our emotional wellbeing can go up and down depending on what is going on in our lives. When things are going well in our lives, the seesaw is perfectly balanced. When things go wrong, and we experience unpleasant or difficult emotions, one end of our seesaw can drop. This can leave us feeling stressed, sad, lonely, worried, overwhelmed. Emotional wellbeing means we can find ways to cope with the challenges life throws at us and rebalance our seesaw.

GROUP ACTIVITY

In your small groups, look at the seesaw below. On one side, write the events, actions or things that can challenge or hurt our emotional wellbeing, or pull us out of balance. On the other side, write the people and actions that can support our emotional wellbeing.

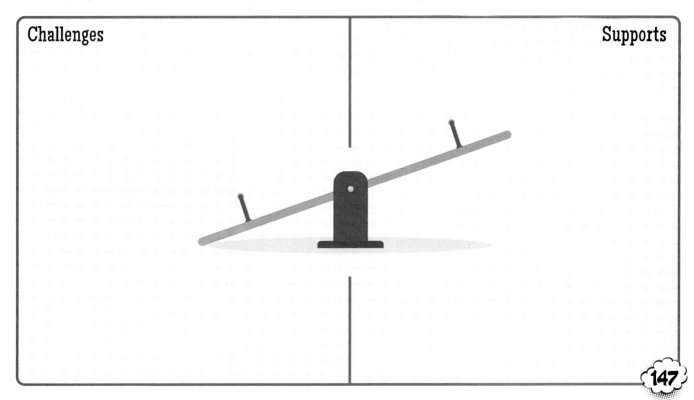

Challenges

Supports

Five-a-Day for Emotional Wellbeing

Connect

Make time each day to connect with people around you at home, in school and in your local community. This can include interacting with your family members and arranging to meet friends. Reducing your screen time when in company can also help you connect with others.

Be active

Evidence shows that there is a link between being physically active and good mental wellbeing. Find activities you enjoy and can fit into your life. Take some time to exercise, go for a walk somewhere you like, cycle with a friend, dance. You may not like traditional gym-type exercise, but there are lots of different physical activities you can try.

Take notice

Take time to stop and become aware of the world around you. Paying attention to our thoughts and feelings can improve our mental health. Stay in the moment, whether you are walking, eating or talking. Being in the moment is also called mindfulness.

Keep learning

Always push yourself to try new things. Take on new responsibilities. Push yourself outside your comfort zone. Learn a new skill, start baking, take up a new hobby, volunteer with an organisation – it doesn't matter what it is, and it doesn't matter how big or small an activity it is. The important thing is to keep trying new things and not to limit yourself or narrow your scope.

Help or support others

Helping and supporting others, or doing small, kind things for them, or even just thanking others and being grateful for what they do for you can be very good for our mental wellbeing. Doing good things for the environment will also have a positive effect on our mental health. So thank someone, or give someone a (sincere) compliment, or do something helpful for someone, even without letting them know it was you who did it. Pick up rubbish and be mindful of your surroundings. Doing these random acts of kindness will not only make others feel better, but they'll make you feel better, too.

INDIVIDUAL ACTIVITY

Now consider each of these areas in relation to your own emotional wellbeing. What are you already doing or what will you do to manage your own emotional wellbeing?

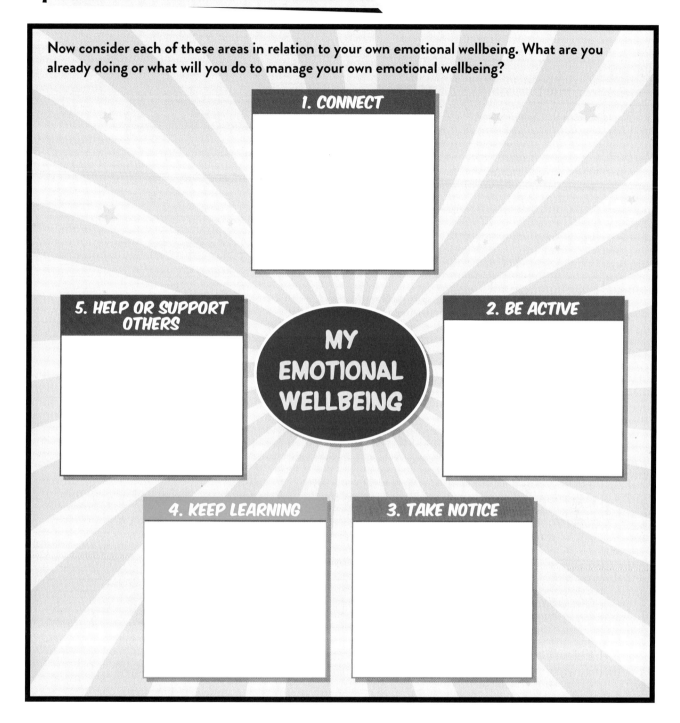

1. CONNECT

5. HELP OR SUPPORT OTHERS

MY EMOTIONAL WELLBEING

2. BE ACTIVE

4. KEEP LEARNING

3. TAKE NOTICE

Getting Help and Support

It is important to remember that we are all different and the way we react to challenging situations can differ from person to person. What one person finds stressful another may not. Life throws things at us sometimes daily that can upset and challenge us, and we all have different ways of coping. If our seesaw is down for too long, we need to ask for help and support from others to feel better. This can be from a parent, carer, teacher, trusted adult or organisation.

INDIVIDUAL ACTIVITY

There are lots of organisations in Ireland that provide support, help and advice for emotional wellbeing if you need it. Match the organisation to its logo by writing the number of the description in the box beside its logo.

#	Description	Logo	
1.	An organisation that delivers services and professional support to children, young and their families. Phone: 01 4530355.	**BODYWHYS** The Eating Disorders Association of Ireland www.bodywhys.ie	☐
2.	A national helpline service for teenagers up to the age of 18 in Ireland. They can be contacted 24 hours a day, 365 days a year. Phone: 1800 833 634.	*Aware* Your supporting light through depression www.aware.ie	☐
3.	A support group for teenagers whose lives have been impacted by a loved one's struggles with alcohol use disorder.	webwise.ie www.webwise.ie	☐
4.	A national charity offering information and support to people affected by eating disorders. Phone: 01 2107906.	JIGSAW Young people's health in mind www.jigsaw.ie	☐
5.	A peer support group for people of all ages who have experienced death, separation or divorce in their lives. Phone: 01473 4175.	www.addictiongroup.org/ treatment/alateen	☐
6.	A national youth support service for gay, lesbian, bisexual and transgender young people. Phone: 01 670 6223.	**Childline** www.childline.ie	☐
7.	A 24-hour helpline and online service offering advice and support to children and young people under 18. Phone: 1800 666 666.	**SVP** Society of St Vincent de Paul www.svp.ie	☐
8.	A free, community-based service for 12–25-year-olds, offering one-on-one support for young people dealing with difficulties.	1800 833 634 **TeenLine** IRELAND www.ispcc.ie/teenline	☐
9.	Offers support and information for anyone experiencing depression. Phone: 1890 303302.	Supporting Lesbian, Gay, Bisexual & Trans Young People in Ireland **belong**TO www.belongto.org	☐
10.	The Irish Internet Safety Awareness Centre, it provides information and advice on online safety issues among young people, their parents and their teachers.	**hotline.ie** www.hotline.ie	☐
11.	A charity dedicated to tackling poverty in all its forms by providing practical assistance to people in need. Phone: 01 884 8200.	spunout **text about it** www.textaboutit.ie	☐
12.	A free, anonymous, 24/7 messaging service providing everything from a calming chat to immediate support for our mental health and emotional wellbeing..	www.barnardos.ie	☐
13.	A free, secure and confidential web-reporting service enabling people to report suspected illegal content online, e.g. non-consensual sharing of intimate images and exploitative content of children and young people.	**Rainbows Ireland** Supporting Children with Bereavement and Parental Separation www.rainbowsireland.ie	☐

INDIVIDUAL ACTIVITY

Your teacher will assign you one of the scenarios below. Read the scenario and answer the questions.

Robert

Robert's parents recently separated. Leading up to the separation, his parents were arguing a lot. Now that Robert's dad has left the family home, his mother is very upset and drinks regularly. He hasn't told anyone about what is going on in his life. He finds it difficult to concentrate at school and it is affecting his grades. He doesn't enjoy doing the things he usually enjoys.

Alex

Alex is in first year at an all boys' secondary school. He is beginning to think he could be gay. He has no interest in girls and doesn't enjoy going to discos, as he feels his friends will put pressure on him to meet a girl. Keeping this secret is making Alex feel unhappy. His parents have no clue that he is feeling this way, and he is afraid of their reaction if he tells them he thinks he is gay. He is unsure who to trust his secret with. He knows a boy in second year who is openly gay, but he knows that he sometimes gets a hard time. Alex doesn't know what to do.

Joanne

Joanne always loved school in primary, but now that she is in secondary school, she is finding it difficult. She is overwhelmed with all the work she has to do. Despite trying her best in class, Joanne is finding schoolwork very difficult. She sometimes gets in trouble in school for poor behaviour or not having her homework completed. When she has an exam coming up, Joanne begins to feel very anxious. Sometimes she pretends she is sick so that she doesn't have to go to school. She hasn't told her parents how she is feeling. When she wakes up in the morning, the thoughts of going to school fill her with dread.

Kayla

Kayla enjoys being on her phone, scrolling through social media or commenting and liking friends' posts. Recently, though, her social media use is making her feel unhappy. She feels unhappy with her own life and appearance when she looks at her friends' posts and celebrity feeds. It seems to her that everyone is having more fun than her and are prettier than her. She often finds herself comparing herself to her friends, who seem to always look good and fit into smaller clothes than her. This is increasingly getting her down. When she looks in the mirror, she sometimes says negative things to herself. She recently started avoiding mealtimes so she can lose weight. This has caused arguments at home. Her mam always tells Kayla she is beautiful, but Kayla just isn't happy with her body.

1. How do you think this person is feeling? _____
_____
_____

2. What could the person do to help improve their situation? _____
_____
_____

3. How might things improve if they got help? _____
_____
_____

4. Why might they be reluctant to ask for help? _____
_____
_____

5. How might things get better if they ask for help? _____
_____
_____

6. What advice would you give this person? _____
_____
_____

7. What organisation could help support them? _____
_____
_____

REFLECTION ON MY LEARNING

What are your body clues that you are upset?
_____
_____
_____

What can you do to make yourself feel better or cheer yourself up if something is upsetting you?
_____
_____
_____

What should you avoid doing when you are upset?
_____
_____
_____

LESSON 24

Recognising and Understanding Emotions and Feelings

Learning Outcomes: 1.9, 4.1, 4.2, 4.3, 4.4

 resilient responsible connected

By the end of this lesson, you will:

→ have explored different emotions and how to recognise them

→ understand that we can express and manage our feelings in helpful and unhelpful ways

→ have explored different coping strategies for managing your feelings and emotions.

 **KEYWORDS**

Emotional wellbeing

Feelings

Body clues

ADDITIONAL RESOURCES

www.childline.ie Childline is a 24-hour helpline and online service that offers advice and support to children and young people under 18. **Freephone: 1800 666 666.**

Text 50808 A free, anonymous 24-hour messaging service that provides everything from a calming chat to immediate support. This text service is a safe space where you are listened to by a trained volunteer. By asking questions, listening to you and responding with support, they will help you sort through your feelings until you both feel you are now in a calm, safe place.

www.ispcc.ie/teenline A national 24-hour helpline service for teenagers up to the age of 18 in Ireland. They can be contacted 24 hours a day, 365 days a year, online or by calling **1800 833 634**.

www.jigsaw.ie Provides information and advice on a range of issues faced by young people.

www.bodywhys.ie Bodywhys is a national charity offering information and support to people affected by eating disorders. **Phone: 01 2107906.**

www.walkinmyshoes.ie Walk in My Shoes is a mental health awareness campaign developed by St Patrick's Mental Health Services. Its website provides resources for young people, such as the Wellbeing Action Calendar, Wellness Journals and Mindful Colouring Sheets.

Feelings and Emotions

A key part of looking after our emotional wellbeing is being able to recognise, name and manage our feelings. Once you have identified your feelings, you can manage them and learn to express them in helpful rather than unhelpful ways. All feelings whether pleasant or unpleasant are valid, they are neither good nor bad. How we express and communicate our feelings with others is important. Strong feelings like anger and fear can sometimes overwhelm us, so once we learn to recognise and regulate these feelings, we can become more in control of how we react in situations, rather than these feelings controlling us.

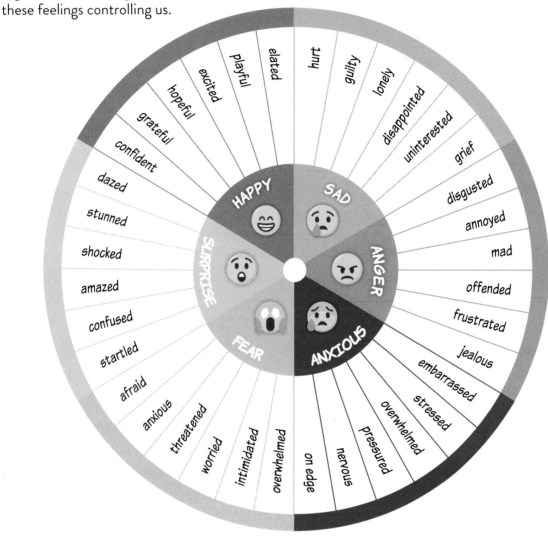

1. I felt _____ when _____

_____

2. I felt _____ when _____

_____

3. I felt _____ when _____

_____

4. I felt _____ when _____

_____

5. I felt _____ when _____

_____

CLASS DISCUSSION

1 Do you think it is OK to feel emotions such as anger, sadness, disgust or jealousy? Why?

2 What would be helpful ways of expressing our emotions?

3 What would be unhelpful ways of expressing our emotions?

4 Do you think boys and girls express their emotions differently? Why?

Understanding Body Clues

Our bodies can give us the best clues as to how we are feeling. For example, if you are nervous, you might get butterflies in your stomach, your muscles might tense up or your heart might start racing. Have you ever heard of the term 'gut feeling'? This is another example of a body clue. It is the instinctive feeling you get inside that something is right or wrong.

INDIVIDUAL ACTIVITY

Look at the different feelings below and write in the different body clues a person may get if they were experiencing this feeling.

A. Happiness

B. Sadness

C. Anger

D. Fear

E. Anxiety

Managing Our Feelings

It is important to be able to recognise our feelings in order to manage them effectively. Paying attention to body clues can play a big part in this. If we can catch out feelings early when they are small and easy to manage, we can prevent them from getting worse. For example, if we start to feel angry in a situation, we can take ourselves away from the situation or count to 10 in our heads. This can give us time to calm down. Or if we are beginning to feel stressed, we can practise deep breathing exercises.

Our Body Thermometer

How we feel will vary in intensity from situation to situation, and the way we respond differs from person to person. Our bodies are a good indicator of the level of intensity of our feelings. We can think of our bodies as our feelings thermometer.

If you had an exam coming up, you might be a little nervous, so you might rate this feeling as 1 or 2 on the scale in terms of intensity. However, having to make a presentation in front of your classmates could make you extremely nervous, and so you might rate this as level 4 or 5 on the thermometer. If you are aware of the intensity of your emotions, you will be in a better position to cope with and manage them.

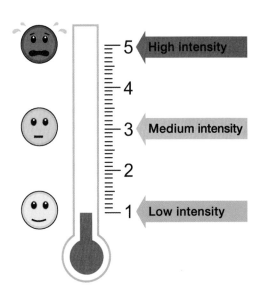

INDIVIDUAL ACTIVITY

Look back on the first activity you did in this lesson ('I felt ... when ...'). In the boxes above each thermometer, rewrite these statements. On the matching thermometer, colour in the thermometer to show the intensity of your feeling. Remember, 1 is low intensity and 5 is high intensity. The higher up you go, the stronger the feeling.

1   2   3   4   5

High intensity

Medium intensity

Low intensity

Don't Bottle It Up

Have you ever dropped a fizzy drinks bottle, picked it up and then opened it, and found the bottle explodes all over you? You probably felt embarrassed or annoyed with yourself, maybe you had to apologise to people nearby who got hit by the spray. Then, after all that, you had to spend time cleaning up the mess!

Now let's imagine our body is that bottle, and the fizzy drink is our feelings. When we allow our feelings to build up inside – when we 'bottle them up' – or if we react when we are caught up in an unpleasant emotion, we may express ourselves in unhelpful ways, such as screaming, slamming doors, crying uncontrollably or isolating ourselves. Afterwards, we can be left regretting our actions.

INDIVIDUAL ACTIVITY

In the bottle to the right, write any intense or difficult feelings you have now or had in the past. Think about the thoughts or events that caused you to have those feelings and how you acted in the situation. You can write them down if you wish, but you don't have to.

While unpleasant emotions, such as anger, fear, sadness, embarrassment, can be very difficult at the time, they are a normal part of life. Our emotions whether pleasant or unpleasant never last forever, they are constantly changing. There is an old saying: 'This too shall pass'. It means that difficult situations don't last forever. What you worried about last week probably doesn't come into your head today.

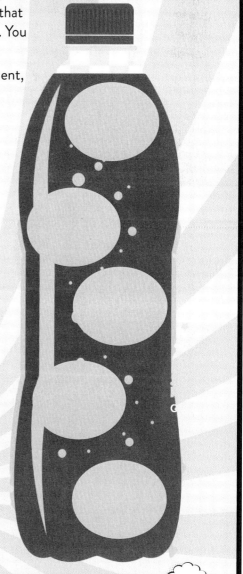

157

Healthy Coping Strategies

We all have unpleasant feelings from time to time, but there are different healthy coping strategies we can use to help us deal with our feelings better. Read the suggestions made by the young people below.

 Emotional regulation refers to our ability to manage or take control of emotions, both pleasant and unpleasant.

When something winds me up and I begin to feel angry, I count down from 10. This helps me to calm down and stops me overreacting and regretting it later.

Walking away from the situation helps me. I take time out on my own. This doesn't solve the problem, but it gives me time to think.

I try to use positive self-talk. I convince myself that the situation will improve, and I will get through it.

My advice would be to talk to someone. I usually talk to my grandad. He is a really good listener and always gives me good advice.

I write a text to the person explaining how I'm feeling and why they have upset me, and then I delete it.

I find music really helps. I have a special playlist that I listen to when I'm feeling upset about something.

Going for a run really helps me to blow off steam. I always feel better after moving.

I go for a walk in a park near my house.

I find screaming into a pillow sometimes helps me to get my feelings out.

I practise some relaxation and breathing exercises that my SPHE teacher told me about. I find these helpful.

I go to a quiet place and get lost in a good book.

I write down what is annoying or worrying me on a piece of paper, then I scrunch it up and throw it away.

Other Helpful Coping Strategies

You might find the following strategies helpful. Remember there is no 'one size fits all' solution for coping, so try to find the coping strategy that works best for you.

Take 5 Breathing Exercise

1. Stretch your hand out like a star.
2. Get your other index finger ready to trace your fingers up and down.
3. Slide up each finger slowly, then down the other side.
4. Breathe in through your nose and out through your mouth.
5. Put it all together. Breathe in as you slide up and breathe out as you slide down. Keep going until you have finished tracing your hand.

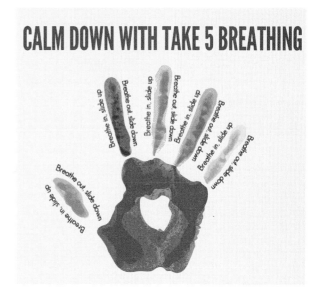

Stay Grounded Exercise

Relax your body, take five deep breaths and focus on the following.

Stay Grounded Using Your 5 Senses

 things you can see

 things you can feel

 things you can hear

 things you can smell

 thing you can taste

Mindful Breathing

When you practise mindful breathing, you can control your emotions by letting your thoughts come and go. This helps you to feel calmer and more in control.

 Go to YouTube and search for 'Mindfulness of the breath' (4:15) by Walk in My Shoes. Watch the video for a mindfulness exercise you can complete on your own or in your class.

INDIVIDUAL ACTIVITY

Using what you have learned in today's lesson and what you think might work best for you, write down some healthy coping strategies you could use to manage more intense emotions.

_____

_____

_____   High intensity → ⎓ 5

_____   ⎓ 4

_____   Medium intensity ⎓ 3

_____   ⎓ 2

_____   Low intensity →   ⎓ 1

_____

REFLECTION ON MY LEARNING

Something that made me think in this lesson was

_____

_____

Healthy ways I could manage my emotions are

_____

_____

_____

Unhealthy ways I could manage my emotions are

_____

_____

_____

LESSON 25

Self-talk: Inner Coach and Inner Critic

Learning Outcomes: 1.9, 4.1, 4.2, 4.4

 resilient aware responsible respected

By the end of this lesson, you will:

•• recognise what is meant by your inner couch and inner critic

•• appreciate the importance of challenging unhelpful thoughts

•• explain the link between our thoughts, feelings and actions.

KEYWORDS

Inner coach

Inner critic

Helpful self-talk

Unhelpful self-talk

ADDITIONAL RESOURCES

www.childline.ie Childline is a 24-hour helpline and online service that offers advice and support to children and young people under 18. **Freephone: 1800 666 666.**

www.ispcc.ie/teenline A national 24-hour helpline service for teenagers up to the age of 18 in Ireland. They can be contacted 24 hours a day, 365 days a year, online or by calling **1800 833 634.**

www.kidshealth.org The teen section of this website provides support and advice for teenagers on health and wellbeing and different aspects of teenage life.

What is Self-talk?

Most of us may not even realise it, but as we go about our day, we have many thoughts chattering away in our heads. Experts estimate that we have between 60,000 to 80,000 thoughts per day! These thoughts are also referred to as 'self-talk'. It is our inner voice that comments on life and what's happening around us. Our self-talk can be helpful as our 'inner coach' or unhelpful as our 'inner critic'.

Unhelpful Self-Talk/Inner Critic

- When you speak to yourself in an unrealistic, hurtful and unhelpful way, which only serves to put you down or make you feel bad about yourself
- Saying judgemental, blaming and discouraging things to yourself which come from your inner critic

Helpful Self-Talk/Inner Coach

- When you speak to yourself in a way that makes you feel good or better about yourself, to be resilient and to work towards achieving your goals
- Saying positive, encouraging, compassionate and supportive things to yourself which come from your inner coach

What might your inner coach and inner critic say in different situations? Read the examples below and see if any of the thoughts are ones you've had yourself.

	Inner critic	Inner coach
1.	I messed up.	I made a mistake, everyone does, I can learn from this.
2.	Everyone in class will see I don't understand if I ask a question about this.	Asking a question will help others too – maybe they are confused also.
3.	I don't have time.	I can set aside time and I will get it done.
4.	I'm not as good as others.	Everyone has strengths and weaknesses. There are many things that I am good at.
5.	No one cares about me.	There are people in my life who will support me.
6.	They would never like me.	I know who my true friends are, and that's what matters.
7.	I don't understand this, I will never get it.	This is hard, but I am going to try my best and keep going.
8.	This is the worst thing ever.	This feels bad now, but with time and support I will get through it.
9.	I'm really nervous about doing this.	I am out of my comfort zone, but it will be worth it.

INDIVIDUAL ACTIVITY

Below are different stresses or challenges young people may experience in their lives. Select one challenge and write an example of self-talk from an inner critic and an example of self-talk from an inner coach for this situation. Can you think of other stresses or challenges that have not been listed? You can choose a challenge from the list or make up your own challenges if you prefer.

Not being invited to a party that everyone in the class has been invited to

Someone posting a nasty comment on an Instagram photo

Being picked as a sub for a match

Getting in trouble in school

Falling out with a friend

Failing an exam

Receiving a bad exam result

Auditioning for a part in the school concert

Taking an exam for a subject you don't enjoy

Asking out someone you fancy

Not getting many likes on a social media post

Feeling unhappy with appearance

Having to stand up and make a presentation in front of a class

Being excluded from a WhatsApp group

Playing badly in a match

Being bullied by a classmate

Finding a subject difficult

Inner critic

Inner coach

The challenge I selected is:

_____

_____

_____

_____

I can't do this.

I will do my best.

The Power of Helpful Self-Talk

Everyone has an inner critic, and we can be very hard on ourselves sometimes. We can say things to ourselves that we would never say to someone we cared about. Saying unhelpful things to ourselves can really impact how we feel about ourselves and our self-esteem. It is important to replace that negative voice in your head with the same type of advice you would offer a friend. Challenging our inner critic and unhelpful thoughts and replacing them with helpful thoughts and listening to our inner coach can have huge benefits for our emotional wellbeing.

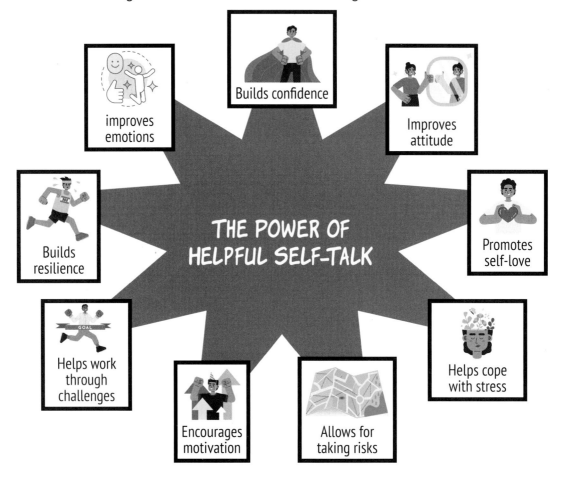

Linking Thoughts, Feelings and Behaviours

How we talk to ourselves can influence how we think and how we feel. Even if we cannot change the situation, we can change the way we think about it and therefore the way we feel and act.

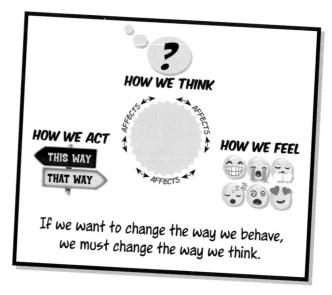

Sally's Self-talk

Sally is 13. She loves creating funny video clips on TikTok and puts a lot of effort into them. She posts one of her videos, eagerly waiting to see the number of likes and comments it receives. She doesn't get as many likes as she expected.

Unhelpful self-talk from an inner critic:

Thoughts
'People must not think I'm funny.'
'I must not be good enough.'

Feelings
Sad
Dejected
Disappointed

Actions
Decides not to make any more videos.
Doubts her abilities.

Helpful self-talk from an inner coach:

Thoughts
'The number of likes doesn't reflect my talent.'
'I know I am good at this, and my friends think I'm funny.'

Feelings
Self-confident
Happy
Proud

Actions
Doesn't dwell on number of likes.
Responds to positive comments she does receive.
Continues to make and post videos because she likes doing it.

INDIVIDUAL ACTIVITY

Look back at the challenge you selected at the start of the lesson, e.g. getting a bad result in a test. In the diagram below, fill in how unhelpful and helpful thoughts in that situation would affect your feelings and actions.

My challenge was _____

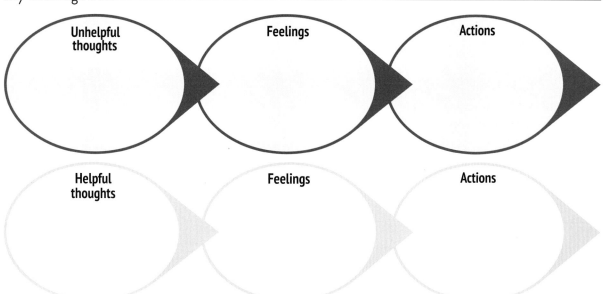

Unhelpful thoughts

Feelings

Actions

Helpful thoughts

Feelings

Actions

Challenging Our Inner Critic

Challenging our inner critic and changing our unhelpful self-talk takes time and practice, but the more we practise, the better we become at noticing it and challenging it, or at least acknowledging and letting it pass by. The more time we spend replacing unhelpful self-talk with helpful self-talk, the more likely we are to manage unpleasant feelings and behaviours, which in turn benefits our emotional wellbeing. Remember that everyone experiences unhelpful self-talk, and everyone – absolutely everyone – experiences difficult scenarios in their lives, sometimes daily! When you have an unhelpful thought, you can challenge the thought by asking yourself the following questions.

Ways to Challenge Unhelpful Self-Talk

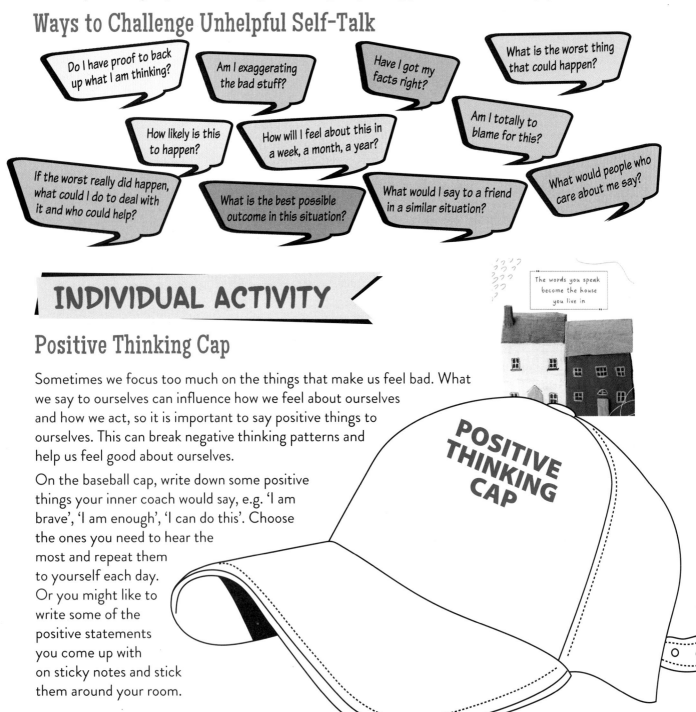

Do I have proof to back up what I am thinking?

Am I exaggerating the bad stuff?

Have I got my facts right?

What is the worst thing that could happen?

How likely is this to happen?

How will I feel about this in a week, a month, a year?

Am I totally to blame for this?

If the worst really did happen, what could I do to deal with it and who could help?

What is the best possible outcome in this situation?

What would I say to a friend in a similar situation?

What would people who care about me say?

The words you speak become the house you live in

INDIVIDUAL ACTIVITY

Positive Thinking Cap

Sometimes we focus too much on the things that make us feel bad. What we say to ourselves can influence how we feel about ourselves and how we act, so it is important to say positive things to ourselves. This can break negative thinking patterns and help us feel good about ourselves.

On the baseball cap, write down some positive things your inner coach would say, e.g. 'I am brave', 'I am enough', 'I can do this'. Choose the ones you need to hear the most and repeat them to yourself each day. Or you might like to write some of the positive statements you come up with on sticky notes and stick them around your room.

POSITIVE THINKING CAP

REFLECTION ON MY LEARNING

During the week, take notice of unhelpful self-talk and replace it with helpful self-talk.

LESSON 26

Digital Wellbeing

Learning Outcomes: 1.9, 2.6, 2.7, 4.5

resilient · connected · aware

By the end of this lesson, you will:

→ recognise the benefits and difficulties associated with being online

→ make changes to manage your screen time

→ understand the benefits of reducing screen time on your health and wellbeing.

KEYWORDS

Screen time

Dopamine

Digital wellbeing

ADDITIONAL RESOURCES

www.childnet.com Offers advice to young people on games and online safety to help you get the best out of the internet and stay safe online.

A large amount of our time now is spent online. We use technology to connect with others, shop, do schoolwork, use social media, play games and watch TV or movies. Having a healthy balance between our time spent online and offline is vital for our overall health and wellbeing.

Digital boundaries are the limits we set ourselves for how much time we want to spend online.

In this lesson, we will explore how much time you spend online and how to balance your online and offline activities.

CLASS ACTIVITY

Stand Up Sit Down

The teacher will call out items from the list below. You have to decide whether you would give up all your electronic devices for a week in exchange for that item. Stand up if you would, stay seated if you wouldn't.

A fast food meal

A bar of chocolate

A packet of crisps

A cinema ticket with food included

A trip to Tayto Park

A pair of new runners

A concert ticket to see your favourite musician

A visit with someone you haven't seen in ages

A drink

A bag of chips

A three-day trip to Disneyland

A ski trip with school friends

A week with no homework

A meal out with your friends followed by bowling

The newest games console

CLASS DISCUSSION

1. How would you cope without your electronic device for a week?

2. What difficulties would you experience most?

3. What would you miss the most?

4. Have you ever gone for a long period of time without devices? How did you feel?

5. In most schools, students are not allowed to use their phones. Do you agree or disagree with this policy? Why do you think this rule exists in schools?

6. What signs do you experience when you have been online too long (signs from your own body, signs from the world around you)?

7. What issues do you think arise for young people who spend too much time on devices?

8. What do you think are the benefits of taking a break from your phone?

9. What do you enjoy about being online? How could you balance the time you spend online with offline activities?

I would give up all my devices for a week in exchange for:

_____

_____

The reason for this is:

_____

_____

INDIVIDUAL ACTIVITY

Devices and Me

Look at the statements below. For each statement, mark where you are on the 'Like me–Not like me' line.

1. I could not guess how much time I spend on devices in a day.
   Like me •━━━━━━━━━━━━━━━━━━━━━━━• Not like me

2. I have stayed up late and lost sleep because I was on a device.
   Like me •━━━━━━━━━━━━━━━━━━━━━━━• Not like me

3. I can leave my phone aside for long periods of time without looking at it.
   Like me •━━━━━━━━━━━━━━━━━━━━━━━• Not like me

4. Someone has commented that I am always on my phone in company.
   Like me •━━━━━━━━━━━━━━━━━━━━━━━• Not like me

5. I have missed conversations with friends and family because of using devices.
   Like me •━━━━━━━━━━━━━━━━━━━━━━━• Not like me

6. I feel hooked on my smartphone, tablet or other devices.
   Like me •━━━━━━━━━━━━━━━━━━━━━━━• Not like me

7. I enjoy spending time on devices – it helps me relax and unwind.
   Like me •━━━━━━━━━━━━━━━━━━━━━━━• Not like me

8. I have used my phone to avoid looking awkward in situations.
   Like me •━━━━━━━━━━━━━━━━━━━━━━━• Not like me

9. My phone use or use of other devices does not get in the way of my homework.
   Like me •━━━━━━━━━━━━━━━━━━━━━━━• Not like me

10. My phone use has prevented me from being in the moment and enjoying an experience because I was too busy recording the event.
    Like me •━━━━━━━━━━━━━━━━━━━━━━━• Not like me

11. I feel the need to check my notifications and scroll social media regularly throughout the day.
    Like me •━━━━━━━━━━━━━━━━━━━━━━━• Not like me

12. I post regularly on my social media feed.
    Like me •━━━━━━━━━━━━━━━━━━━━━━━• Not like me

13. The number of likes I get on a post is very important to me.
    Like me •━━━━━━━━━━━━━━━━━━━━━━━• Not like me

14. I feel sometimes I am missing out when I see what other people are posting online.
    Like me •━━━━━━━━━━━━━━━━━━━━━━━• Not like me

What do you think this activity tells you about your technology use?

_____

_____

What are the positives and negatives for you of the amount of time you spend on devices each day?

_____

_____

FOMO and Dopamine

Have you ever felt that you have to keep looking at your phone because you don't want to miss out on anything? If this is the case, you may be experiencing FOMO (Fear of Missing Out). Like addictive substances, being online, gaming, chatting or scrolling through your social media feed stimulates your brains to release dopamine. Dopamine is a chemical controlled by your brain's reward centre. When dopamine is released, it makes us feel good. Our brains want more dopamine, which triggers the habit of checking our phones constantly throughout the day. The good news is that limiting your screen time can have a positive impact on your health and wellbeing.

Less stress. Less time spent playing video games, checking your calls, texts, scrolling social media updates can reduce your stress.

Improved sleep. Limiting screen time two hours before you plan to go to bed helps you fall asleep more easily and improves your sleep quality.

Better connections with friends and family. When you put your phone away, you'll improve your relationships because you'll be able to spend more, better quality time with others.

BENEFITS OF LIMITING SCREEN TIME

More gratitude. As we spend less time comparing ourselves to others, wishing we had what others have, and we are more grateful for what we have.

Delayed gratification. Online activities offer us instant rewards and satisfaction. Delaying the impulse to look at our phones and devices can result in us being able to be more controlled and less impulsive in other areas of our lives.

Improved creativity. If we don't rely on the internet for information, we can use our brains and become more creative and resourceful.

INDIVIDUAL ACTIVITY

A Day in the Life of a Device

The battery below represents the battery on your phone or device. If you normally use your phone or device during any one of the times/activities scattered around the battery, colour in one section of the battery.

On the toilet

In the shower

As soon as you wake up

Talking to friends

When walking to school

On the bus or train

Doing sports

Eating dinner

When out for a run or walk

During break or lunchtime

Doing homework

Watching TV

Talking to family

In bed

+

−

CLASS DISCUSSION

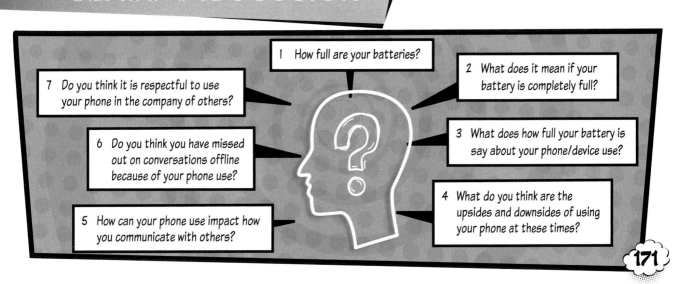

1   How full are your batteries?

2   What does it mean if your battery is completely full?

7   Do you think it is respectful to use your phone in the company of others?

3   What does how full your battery is say about your phone/device use?

6   Do you think you have missed out on conversations offline because of your phone use?

5   How can your phone use impact how you communicate with others?

4   What do you think are the upsides and downsides of using your phone at these times?

171

CLASS ACTIVITY

Your teacher will ask you now to give a show of hands for each time someone in the class used their phone. Record these results in the table below and represent them on the bar graph.

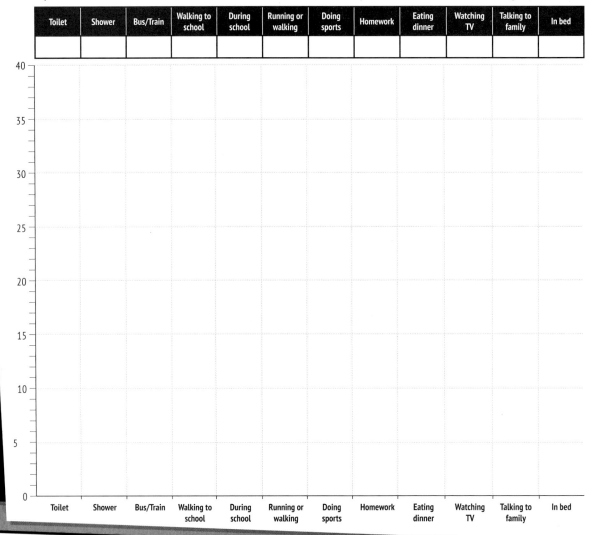

Toilet	Shower	Bus/Train	Walking to school	During school	Running or walking	Doing sports	Homework	Eating dinner	Watching TV	Talking to family	In bed

CLASS DISCUSSION

5 What are the positive and negative influences of phone use on our ability to communicate with others, both online and offline?

1 What did you notice about the times classmates use their phones?

2 Did anything in particular stand out?

4 What was the least common time someone used their phone?

3 What was the most common time someone used their phone?

Managing your online wellbeing

Sometimes we may be unaware of the amount of time we spend online. There are many small changes or activities we can do to reduce this. In your small group, brainstorm what we can do to reduce our screen time.

HOW TO REDUCE SCREEN TIME

REFLECTION ON MY LEARNING

Make the Change: Reduce Your Screen Time

If you are spending a lot of time on devices, it may be time to make some small changes in your life. Making these small changes can help you improve your health and wellbeing by allowing you to have a healthy balance of activities in your life.

A small change I would make to reduce my screen time is:

_____

_____

I would do this because:

_____

_____

If you don't spend a lot of time online, think about what habits or activities helped you maintain this.

A habit or activity that has helped me maintain a healthy level of screen time is:

_____

_____

I found this helped because:

_____

_____

UNIT 6

HEALTHY CHOICES

LESSON 27

Being Healthy

Learning Outcomes: 2.1, 2.4

active   responsible   resilient   aware

By the end of this lesson, you will:

- understand what being healthy looks like
- appreciate what might influence your health-related choices
- recognise reliable and less reliable sources of information on health and wellbeing.

ADDITIONAL RESOURCES

www.kidshealth.org The teen section of this website provides support and advice for teenagers on health and wellbeing and different aspects of teenage life.

KEYWORDS

Health

Healthy choices

Influences

Physical

Social

Emotional

Health Triangle

Being Healthy

Being healthy is more than just not being ill. It is about taking care of our minds and bodies so that we feel our best and live productive and fulfilled lives. To stay healthy, we have to make smart choices in our lives and develop lifelong habits that promote our overall wellbeing.

GROUP ACTIVITY

Using the pictures below as prompts, write down what a first-year student should do to 'be healthy'.

The Health Triangle

The Health Triangle is a good visual to help us understand three major aspects of our overall health:

- physical health
- emotional health
- social health.

Like an equilateral triangle must have balance in each side, having balance in all three areas of our health is essential to living a healthy lifestyle. Neglecting one aspect of our health can have an impact on our overall wellbeing.

Emotional health is understanding and expressing our feelings appropriately. Everyone experiences disappointments or setbacks; having good emotional health is about being able to cope with these disappointments in our lives and bouncing back from them. It is also about knowing when and how to ask for help when we need it.

EMOTIONAL

HEALTH

SOCIAL

Social health is about how we relate to and get on with other people in our lives. It is about building and maintaining healthy relationships that make us feel good about ourselves. It means spending time with our family and friends and other people in our community and having respect, empathy and tolerance for other people. When we have good social health, we feel connected and supported by other people in our lives.

PHYSICAL

Physical health involves taking care of our bodies so we can feel good and have the energy to do things we enjoy. Physical health is not just about how you look but how you feel inside. We can look after our physical health by eating healthily, taking regular exercise, sleeping well and avoiding things that harm our bodies like smoking, drinking alcohol or using drugs.

Achieving the Balance

In order to look after our overall health, all three sides of our triangle need to be balanced. Answer the questions in the table to examine how healthy you are.

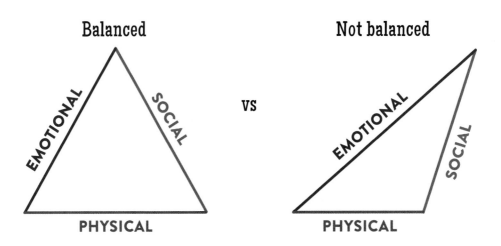

Balanced vs Not balanced

INDIVIDUAL ACTIVITY

Answer the questions in the table below to examine how healthy you are. For every 'yes' answer, give yourself a score of 1.

	PHYSICAL HEALTH STATEMENTS	YES	NO
1	I get at least eight hours of sleep each night.		
2	I generally eat a well-balanced diet, which includes a healthy breakfast.		
3	I have good hygiene practices, e.g. brushing my teeth, washing my hands before eating, and having regular showers or baths.		
4	I do at least 60 minutes of some form of physical activity each day.		
5	I avoid the use of nicotine, alcohol and other drugs.		
6	I see a doctor and dentist for regular checkups.		
	Total:		

	EMOTIONAL HEALTH STATEMENTS	YES	NO
1	I ask for help when I need it, and I know where to get it.		
2	I can express my feelings (hurt, sadness, fear, anger, joy) in a healthy way.		
3	I get along with the people in my life.		
4	I generally feel good about myself.		
5	I like to learn new things and develop new skills.		
6	I have strategies to help me cope with tough times.		
	Total:		

	SOCIAL HEALTH STATEMENTS	YES	NO
1	I have a healthy balance between my time spent online and the connections with family and friends in the real world.		
2	I am a good listener, and I try to put myself in other people's shoes.		
3	I am able to say 'no' if people ask me to do things I think will be harmful or dangerous.		
4	I think I have a good balance between my school, work and social life.		
5	I show respect and care for my family and friends.		
6	I can disagree with others and allow others to disagree with me without getting angry.		
	Total:		
	Grand Total:		

Drawing Your Health Triangle

You are now going to draw your Health Triangle based on your answers to the previous activity. For example, If you gave yourself a score of 5 for physical health, mark 5 on the physical axis below. Repeat this for each side of the Health Triangle. Once you have marked all three axes, draw a triangle connecting the three points to make the Health Triangle.

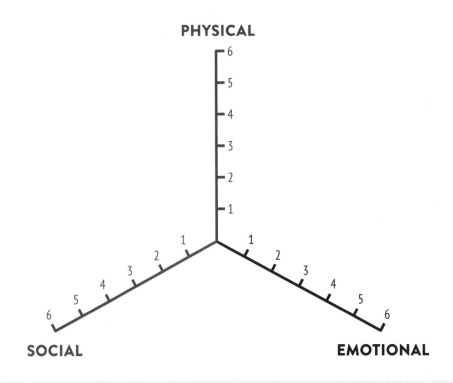

Analysing Your Health Triangle

1. Does your Health Triangle have equal sides? Yes ☐ No ☐

2. Is there any area of your health that you are particularly strong in?

   _____

3. From answering the questionnaire and completing the Health Triangle, as well as what you have learned about health, can you think of any area of your health you could improve on? What changes could you make to improve this area of your health?

   _____

   _____

   _____

4. What have you learned from completing this activity?

   _____

   _____

   _____

Influences on Our Health

GROUP ACTIVITY

Each of the images below represents a different influence on our health-related choices. In groups, discuss how each one could influence the healthy and unhealthy choices we make in our lives. Once you have done this, rank them on the ladder from the least influential to the most influential.

Religions and beliefs

Government campaigns

MOST INFLUENTIAL

Advertisements
(e.g. TV, online, billboards, magazines)

Media
(e.g. news reports)

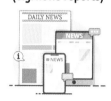

School and teachers

Family and culture

Celebrities

Role models
(e.g. parents, celebrities, athletes)

Social media
(e.g. influencers, viral posts)

Scientific findings

Friends and peers

LEAST INFLUENTIAL

CLASS DISCUSSION

1 What do you think has the strongest influence on the unhealthy choices we make? Why?

2 What do you think has the strongest influence on the healthy choices we make? Why?

3 What do you think are the different challenges to staying healthy? How can we overcome these challenges?

4 How might we be affected differently by the same influence?

5 What influence might be more difficult to manage?

6 How do you think peer influence impacts our decisions to make healthy choices? How can we resist this pressure?

7 Which influence do you think is the most and least reliable source of information about health and wellbeing? Why?

GROUP ACTIVITY

Making Healthy Choices

Each of the people below have a choice to make about their health. From what you learned in class today, give them three pieces of advice to help them make healthy choices.

> I'm playing so many sports I'm finding it really difficult to get the balance between sports, homework and sleep.

> A lot of my friends are vaping in the school bathrooms. I feel increased pressure to join in.

> I have started to get a lot of spots lately. I saw an influencer on social media who had flawless skin after using a cream. I'm thinking of buying it.

> I'm spending a lot of time gaming with my friends. I don't get as much exercise now and I've developed unhealthy eating patterns while doing it.

> I am not able to eat breakfast in the morning. I usually buy sausage rolls and an energy drink before school to help boost my energy during the day.

> I am always comparing myself to the girls I see online. I wish I could look like them.

> I struggle to get up in the morning because I stay up late on my phone.

> The disco is on Saturday night. I know some of my friends will be asking me to bring drinks.

> My appetite has really increased lately, and I'm finding myself eating a lot of convenience food.

REFLECTION ON MY LEARNING

3 things I learned

2 things I found interesting

1 question I am left with

LESSON 28

Healthy Eating

Learning Outcomes: 2.1, 2.2

By the end of this lesson, you will:

- appreciate the importance of healthy food choices to your overall health and wellbeing
- understand how to eat a healthy balanced diet
- have investigated how unhealthy foods are advertised and marketed.

KEYWORDS

Balanced diet

Food pyramid

Advertising

ADDITIONAL RESOURCES

www.safefood.net Safefood provides information and tips on nutrition and food safety.

www.hse.ie Search 'healthy eating guidelines' for up-to-date information on healthy eating.

www.bordbia.ie Bordbia gives detailed information on healthy eating and the food pyramid.

Healthy Eating

During our teenage years, our bodies and minds are developing and growing quickly. Eating a balanced diet that includes a variety of fruits, vegetables, whole grains and lean protein plays an essential role in our overall health and wellbeing.

GROUP ACTIVITY

In small groups, discuss and write down what you think are the benefits of eating healthily to your overall health and wellbeing.

BENEFITS OF EATING HEALTHILY

INDIVIDUAL ACTIVITY

Look at the statement below and mark on the scale where you stand in relation to this.

'It is easy to eat healthily.'

Strongly disagree ← 1   2   3   4   5   6   7   8   9   10 → **Strongly agree**

CLASS DISCUSSION

1 What influenced where you marked the scale?

2 Do you think friends and peers influence our food choices?

3 What do you think influences someone to eat healthily?

4 What do you think influences unhealthy food choices?

5 What are some of the ways that social media and advertising influence young people's food choices?

6 How do you think a person's family or cultural background could influence their food choices?

The Food Pyramid

The food pyramid is a visual representation of recommended food groups and serving sizes that can help us eat a healthy and balanced diet. It is for adults, teenagers and children aged five and over.

It organises foods into five main shelves. The idea is that we should eat more of the foods from the bottom shelves and less of the foods from the top shelves.

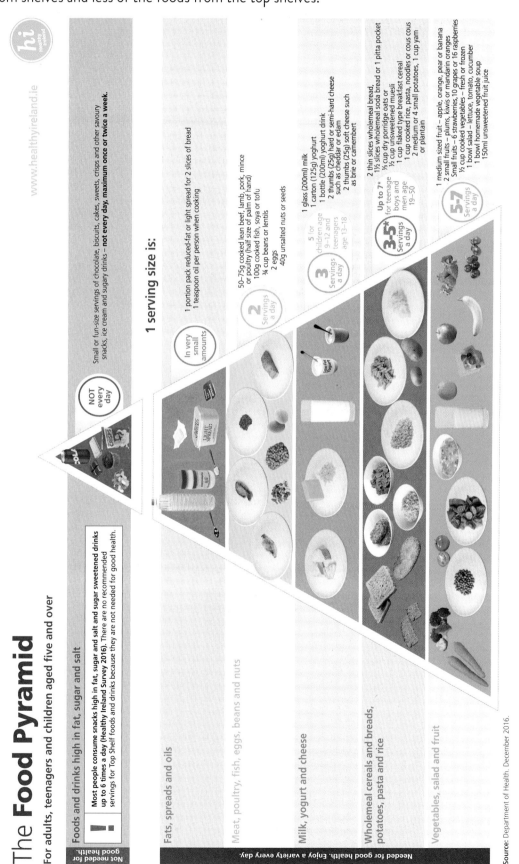

Source: Department of Health. December 2016.

INDIVIDUAL ACTIVITY

What Foods Do

Listed below in the middle are the different food groups which make up the food pyramid and are part of a healthy balanced diet. Match these with their function by drawing a line from the food group to its function.

Your body needs these but only in small amounts. They help provide energy, keep you warm and help you absorb certain vitamins. Saturated varieties are unhealthy. Foods labelled polyunsaturated or monounsaturated are healthier for our hearts. Use these sparingly.

These are sometimes described as 'junk food'. Try to avoid these foods or limit them to a treat once or twice a week. There are no recommended servings for these, because they are not needed for good health. Eating too much of this food group can cause tooth decay and weight gain.

It is recommended that you eat five portions of these a day. They are an important source of vitamins and minerals. They contain fibre, which aids digestion and prevents constipation. They are low in calories and can be a good source of water. They are a good option as a healthy snack.

Vegetables, salads and fruit

Wholemeal cereals and breads, potatoes, pasta and rice

Milk, yoghurt and cheese

Meat, poultry, fish, eggs, beans and nuts

Fats, spreads and oils

Foods and drinks high in fat, sugar and salt

These are rich in calcium, needed for healthy bones and teeth. They provide protein to help growth and repair of our bodies and boost our immune system, which protects us from illness.

This food group is rich in protein, which helps growth and repair of body tissue. They also contain vitamins and minerals. One food is a great source of iron for healthy blood. It is important to choose lean options and limit processed varieties of these.

These foods are a good source of carbohydrates, which help to give us energy. Servings can depend on activity levels and gender. Whole grain or wholemeal options are the better option as they contain more fibre, which moves food more easily through the body. They also allow us to feel full for longer by providing a steady release of energy. They can be eaten at each meal.

Helping Hands: Serving Sizes

We often know what to eat but not how much. Our hands are the perfect measuring device to help us understand what a serving size of each food group is.

Clenched fist

A serving size of cereals, bread, pasta, rice

Palm

A serving size of meat, fish, chicken

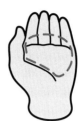

One handful

A serving size of fruits, nuts, raisins

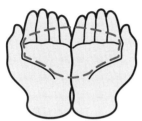

Two handfuls

A serving size of vegetables, salads

Thumb

A serving size of cheese, peanut butter (approx. 1 tbsp)

Tip of thumb

A serving size of butter, mayonnaise, salad dressing (approx. 1 tsp)

INDIVIDUAL ACTIVITY

Healthy Eating and Me

Write down everything you ate and drank yesterday.

BREAKFAST	LUNCH	DINNER

MID-MORNING SNACK	AFTERNOON SNACK	EVENING SNACK

DRINKS

1. Look again at what you ate yesterday. Write or draw what you ate on the correct shelf of your own food pyramid. (For example, if you ate a 125g yoghurt, write or draw a carton of yoghurt on the 'Milk, yoghurt and cheese' shelf. This would represent one serving of this food group.) Remember to include any snacks you had during the day. Some foods contain ingredients from a few shelves, e.g. pizza. In this instance, place the different food types contained in that item on the different shelves.

2. When you have finished filling in your food pyramid, add up the total number of servings you had for each shelf and place them in the box beside the shelf. Compare these to the servings recommended by the food pyramid on the previous page.

3. Fill in how many glasses of water you had in the glass.

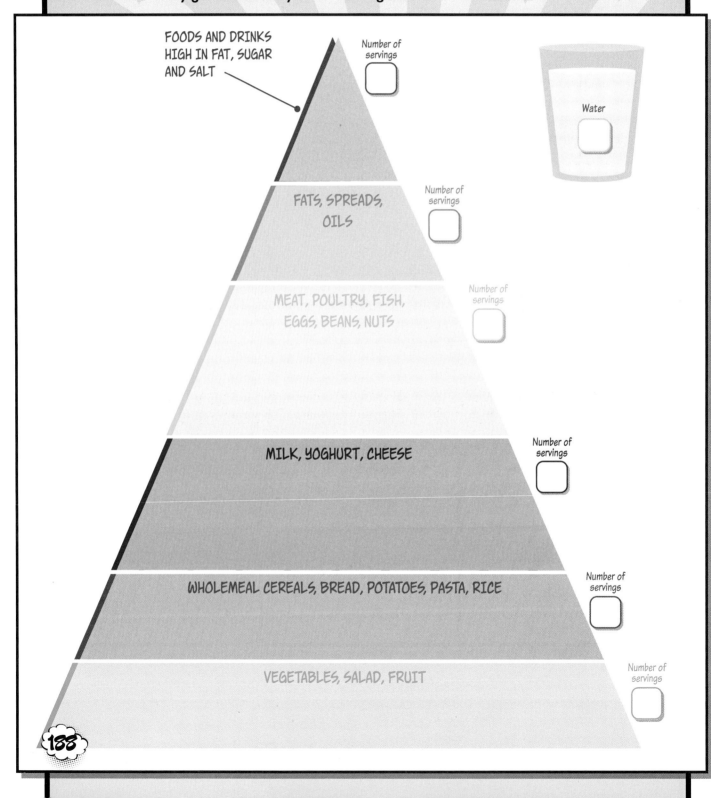

FOODS AND DRINKS HIGH IN FAT, SUGAR AND SALT

Number of servings

Water

FATS, SPREADS, OILS

Number of servings

MEAT, POULTRY, FISH, EGGS, BEANS, NUTS

Number of servings

MILK, YOGHURT, CHEESE

Number of servings

WHOLEMEAL CEREALS, BREAD, POTATOES, PASTA, RICE

Number of servings

VEGETABLES, SALAD, FRUIT

Number of servings

4. Based on your food pyramid, answer these questions:

    (a) What does your pyramid tell you about your diet?

    _____

    _____

    (b) Are there any food groups from which you are eating too much?

    _____

    _____

    (c) Are there any food groups from which you are eating too little?

    _____

    _____

5. Use the food pyramid guidelines to create your own healthy daily meal plan. Write down what you choose to eat for each mealtime below. Remember to have the recommended number of servings for each food group. Write down the number of servings of each food group you select to ensure you achieve the recommended daily amount of each food group.

    Name: _____

    Age: _____

    Level of activity (daily/weekly, etc.): _____

BREAKFAST	LUNCH	DINNER

MID-MORNING SNACK	AFTERNOON SNACK	EVENING SNACK

    DRINKS

Tips for Healthy Eating

Eat a healthy breakfast

Eating a healthy breakfast sets you up for the day. Include whole grains, proteins and fruits in your breakfast.

Save sugary drinks and snacks for treats

Cut back on sugary sodas, energy drinks and juices in your day-to-day diet. Instead, choose water, unsweetened beverages and whole fruits for snacks.

Limit processed and fast foods

Reduce the number of processed foods you eat like crisps, biscuits, ready-made meals and fast food. They are often high in unhealthy fats, added sugars and salt.

Get your five-a-day

Aim to eat at least five servings of fruit and vegetables each day.

Eat regular meals

Try not to leave more than four or five hours between meals. Hunger can cause us to make unhealthy food choices.

Drink plenty of water

Stay hydrated by drinking water throughout the day. It is recommended to drink the equivalent of eight to ten glasses of water per day. Water is important for digestion, concentration and overall health. Bring a water bottle to school and refill it when needed.

Choose whole grains

Choose whole grain bread, rice, pasta and cereals instead of refined or white grains. Whole grains are better for us and help us to feel fuller for longer.

Watch portion sizes

Pay attention to portion sizes to avoid overeating or undereating. Try to listen to your body's hunger and fullness cues.

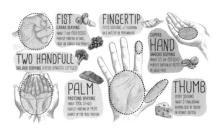

Limit salt intake

Keep an eye on the amount of salt you put on your food. Taste your food before adding salt. Try other healthier flavourings such as pepper, spices and herbs if you think it needs more flavour.

Prepare your lunch

Take responsibility for preparing your own lunches the night before school. This means you won't have to go to the shop or school canteen, where it's more likely that you'll make unhealthy choices.

Eat healthy snacks

Choose nutritious snacks like yoghurt, fresh fruits, nuts or veggie sticks with hummus. Avoid reaching for sugary snacks or chips when you feel hungry between meals.

Avoid emotional eating

Pay attention to how you feel when you eat. Avoid using food as a way of dealing with stress, boredom or sadness. Instead, cheer yourself up with a call to a friend, some gentle exercise or your favourite hobby.

Cut down on added sugar

It is recommended that we limit our sugar intake to around six teaspoons per day. Unfortunately, there is hidden sugar in foods that we eat, so it can be easy to exceed that amount without realising it. For example, sauces such as tomato ketchup, brown sauce and even mayonnaise can contain a lot of sugar. Check the labels to stay informed on what you're eating.

Food Advertising and Marketing

Whether we realise it or not, we are constantly being bombarded with advertisements about food. You have probably seen food advertisements on social media, billboards, television, radio, signs at sports events, bus shelters, sports jerseys, influencers and other forms. These advertisements can influence how we think and what we buy either consciously or unconsciously. The manufacturers want to sell their product to young people, so they have a variety of clever marketing and advertising techniques to make unhealthy products look tempting or necessary to us. Understanding the clever, persuasive techniques used by advertisers can help us not fall for their tricks and make healthy food choices.

Marketing Techniques

Influencers

Influencers are just normal people, but their large followings can gain them celebrity status. Influencers' recommendations and opinions can therefore have an impact on a lot of people. Marketing companies use this influence by asking influencers to promote their products. You may not realise it, but the influencer is paid to promote the product. An example might be an influencer posting pictures of themselves enjoying a particular brand of fizzy drink or sugary snack. They might emphasise how delicious and satisfying these treats are, which can influence their followers to buy these products. It is important to remember that just because an influencer promotes a product, it doesn't mean it is good for you!

Erik the Electric takes on an AMCAP ('as many calories as possible') challenge on social media

Product Placement

Product placement is a marketing tactic where products or brands are placed in movies, TV shows or even interviews. The marketing companies pay to have their product on display. The goal is to make the viewer notice the product and remember it. This creates a positive association between the product and the movie you like or the athlete you admire, which can influence you to buy the product. This can be very subtle like a brand or a logo in the

Diet Coke features in comedy movie Clueless

background or an actor or athlete using the product. Can you think of any examples?

Discounts or Affordable Prices

Marketing companies use the fact that young people may not have a lot of money to entice young people to buy their products. Unhealthy products are often cheap and affordable for young people. Bundle deals like 'two for the price of one' may encourage young people to buy a product as they think they are getting more value for their money. Fast food chains also promote affordable meal deals.

Irish Heart Foundation
The National Stroke & Heart Charity

The Irish Heart Foundation has created a series of video clips to help young people understand how marketing companies target young people. Go to YouTube, find the Irish Heart Foundation channel and click on the 'Stop Targeting Kids' playlist to see some of the tactics that companies use to target you.

GROUP ACTIVITY

Below are a number of clever advertising tricks used by manufacturers to sell products. In your group, try to think of an advertisement you have seen recently that uses this technique.

Catchy names/slogans/jingles/songs
Using catchy names, slogans, jingles or songs to help to keep the product in our memory.

Product example: _____

Fear of missing out (FOMO)
Convincing the consumer that other people are using the product and they should join the crowd. The suggestion is you will be left out if you don't join the crowd and use the product.

Product example: _____

Promise of a better life
Convincing the consumer that if they buy this product, their lives will be like the person in the advertisement, e.g. they will have lots of fun, they will have lots of friends.

Product example: _____

Packaging
Using bright, colourful packaging to capture young people's sense of fun.

Product example: _____

Freebies
The promise of getting something for free if you buy the produc, for example coupons, games, toys from most recent popular cartoons.

Product example: _____

Cartoon characters
A cartoon character or animation is used in the advertisement, making the product more attractive to the young person.

Product example: _____

INDIVIDUAL ACTIVITY

Go to YouTube and search for 'Compilation of Junk Food Commercials Aimed at Children and Teens' (4:18). For each of the adverts featured, decide what advertising or marketing technique is being used to encourage young people to buy the product. There may be more than one technique in each advert!

Advert 1: The advertising technique used is _____.

Advert 2: The advertising technique used is _____.

Advert 3: The advertising technique used is _____.

Advert 4: The advertising technique used is _____.

Advert 5: The advertising technique used is _____.

Advert 6: The advertising technique used is _____.

Advert 7: The advertising technique used is _____.

Advert 8: The advertising technique used is _____.

Advert 9: The advertising technique used is _____.

Advert 10: The advertising technique used is _____.

REFLECTION ON MY LEARNING

Three ways I can make healthy food choices in my life are:

1. _____

_____

2. _____

_____

3. _____

_____

LESSON 29

Physical Activity

Learning Outcomes: 1.5, 2.1

active   aware   responsible

By the end of this lesson, you will:

→ investigate how physical activity contributes to your overall health and wellbeing

→ set goals to improve or maintain your level of physical activity.

KEYWORDS

Recommended
Moderate activity
Vigorous activity
Strength
Flexibility
Gender stereotyping

ADDITIONAL RESOURCES

www.hersport.ie Hersport is a digital media channel dedicated to promoting gender stereotyping in sports. Striving to ensure women the same opportunities as men, they provide daily content, including videos, podcasts, newsletters and social media posts.

www.getirelandactive.ie An Irish website promoting the importance of having an active lifestyle, providing useful tips on how to get and stay active.

As well as a healthy diet, regular physical activity along with adequate rest and sleep are very important to overall health and wellbeing. Regular physical activity contributes not only to a healthy, well-functioning body, both inside and out, but also to a healthy mind, while adequate downtime and sleep promote recovery – all important factors in promoting physical and mental wellbeing.

INDIVIDUAL ACTIVITY

Physical Activity: Myth or Fact?

CLASS DISCUSSION

1 Was there anything that surprised you from doing this quiz?

2 What are some of the factors that influence young people's activity levels?

3 What do you think are the main challenges to getting 60 minutes of exercise each day?

4 Did the answers to questions 4 and 7 surprise you? How do you think gender stereotyping impacts young women's activity levels?

5 Are there equal supports and resources for female and male athletes?

6 Can you think of different ways we can reduce gender stereotyping in sport?

GROUP ACTIVITY

Benefits of Physical Activity

Physical activity has many benefits for our overall health and wellbeing. As a group, come up with as many benefits of physical activity as you can think of. Write them in the box.

Benefits of physical activity

Physical Activity Challenges

In small groups, discuss three challenges to staying physically active that you might face and how these can be overcome.

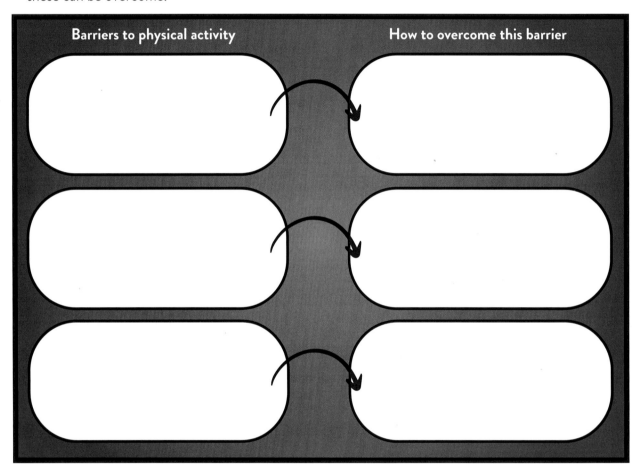

Barriers to physical activity | How to overcome this barrier

INDIVIDUAL ACTIVITY

1. Measure your heart rate before exercise now, using the pulse in your wrist or in your neck.

   My heart rate before exercise is _____ beats per minute (bpm).

2. On your teacher's command, you are now going to jog on the spot for two minutes. As soon as you stop, you will measure your heart rate again.

   My heart rate immediately after exercise is _____ bpm.

3. How has your heart rate changed?

   _____

4. What other differences did you notice in your body after the activity?

   _____

Your resting heart rate is the number of beats per minute of your heart when it is at complete rest. It is best to take your resting heart rate first thing in the morning. As you get fitter, your resting heart rate should decrease. This is because your heart gets more efficient at pumping blood around the body. At rest, more blood can be pumped around with each beat, so fewer beats are needed to supply your body with enough blood and oxygen.

During physical activity, your heart beats faster to pump more blood (and the oxygen that it carries) to the working muscles. Like any muscle, the heart needs to be exercised to become stronger. Any exercise that raises your heart rate and makes you feel warm helps to strengthen your heart. It is recommended that you do 60 minutes of physical activity every day at a moderate to vigorous intensity level to stay healthy.

Moderate intensity	Vigorous intensity
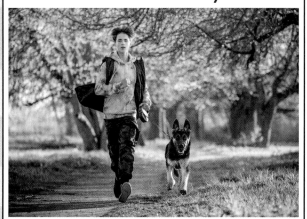	
When exercising at a moderate intensity level: • your breathing is quicker than normal, but you are not out of breath • you develop a light sweat after about 10 minutes • you could carry out a conversation, but you wouldn't be able to sing • Your heart beats faster than normal.	When exercising at a vigorous intensity level: • your breathing is deep and rapid • you start sweating a few minutes into the activity • you can only say a few words without taking a breath • it's difficult to hold a conversation • your heart beats much faster than normal.

The Activity Pyramid

It is recommended that adolescents do at least 60 minutes of moderate to vigorous intensity exercise every day. This can include aerobic activities such as running, walking and playing sports, as well as exercises that improve strength, balance, flexibility and bone strength.

INDIVIDUAL ACTIVITY

The Physical Activity Pyramid shows different ways to stay active and how often you need to exercise to stay fit and healthy. In the blank boxes next to the pyramid on the next page, write what activity you participate in and how often you do it. Then answer the questions.

The Physical Activity Pyramid

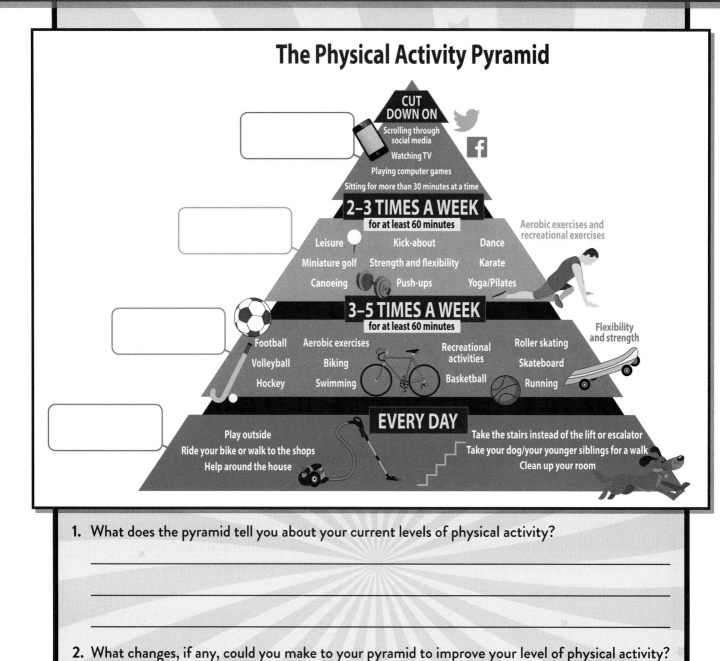

CUT DOWN ON
- Scrolling through social media
- Watching TV
- Playing computer games
- Sitting for more than 30 minutes at a time

2–3 TIMES A WEEK
for at least 60 minutes

Aerobic exercises and recreational exercises

- Leisure
- Kick-about
- Dance
- Miniature golf
- Strength and flexibility
- Karate
- Canoeing
- Push-ups
- Yoga/Pilates

3–5 TIMES A WEEK
for at least 60 minutes

Flexibility and strength

- Football
- Aerobic exercises
- Recreational activities
- Roller skating
- Volleyball
- Biking
- Skateboard
- Hockey
- Swimming
- Basketball
- Running

EVERY DAY

- Play outside
- Ride your bike or walk to the shops
- Help around the house
- Take the stairs instead of the lift or escalator
- Take your dog/your younger siblings for a walk
- Clean up your room

1. What does the pyramid tell you about your current levels of physical activity?

_____

_____

_____

2. What changes, if any, could you make to your pyramid to improve your level of physical activity?

_____

_____

INDIVIDUAL ACTIVITY

1. In order to achieve the recommended daily amount of physical activity, it is important to set goals. You are now going to draw up a physical activity plan for the next week. Before you draw up your plan, note the following:
   - You do not have to do the recommended 60 minutes per day all at once; you can break it up into shorter bouts over the course of the day. For example:
     - Cycling to school = 15 mins
     - Playing basketball at break = 15 mins
     - Having a kick-about = 10 mins
     - Vacuuming your bedroom = 5 mins
     - Walking your dog = 15 mins

- Choose activities that you enjoy doing.
- If you are not normally physically active, start slowly and build up to the 60 minutes.
- Taking part in regular physical activity with a friend can help keep you motivated.
- Keep track of your progress and tick off the activities as you do them.

2. Now, in the physical activity planner below, write in the activities you plan to do for the next week and how much time you plan to spend on each activity. Record your progress and say how you felt after each activity.

My Physical Activity Planner

	Activities I plan to do	Level on the physical activity pyramid	Planned time	How I did
Monday				
Tuesday				
Wednesday				
Thursday				
Friday				
Saturday				
Sunday				

REFLECTION ON MY LEARNING

On the scale below, rate your physical activity.

Very poor ←――――――――――――→ Excellent
1   2   3   4   5   6   7   8   9   10

Three things I learned in this lesson:

1. _____

_____

2. _____

_____

3. _____

_____

As a result of this lesson, I will _____

_____

LESSON 30

The Importance of Sleep

Learning Outcome: 2.1

resilient   aware

By the end of this lesson, you will:

•➜ appreciate the importance of a good night's sleep to your overall health and wellbeing

•➜ develop strategies to help get a good night's sleep

•➜ evaluate your own sleep habits and make improvements.

KEYWORDS

Melatonin

Sleep routine

Circadian rhythm

ADDITIONAL RESOURCES

www.kidshealth.org Provides information and advice on sleep.

Sometimes, we can underestimate the importance of sleep to our health and wellbeing. Sleep is just as important as having a healthy diet and exercising. It is recommended that teenagers get 8–10 hours of sleep every night. In this lesson, you will examine the sleep habits of people in your class, learn what affects a good night's sleep and develop strategies to get a good sleep routine.

Rate Your Sleep

How good is your sleep routine? Mark on the scale how you would rate your sleep routine.

EXCELLENT

POOR

GROUP ACTIVITY

Benefits of a Good Sleep Routine

In your small groups, discuss the impact of a good sleep routine on a young person's health and wellbeing. Write down your ideas in the graphic below.

Sleep-Walking Bingo

CLASS ACTIVITY

The following activity will allow you to find out about the sleep habits of people in your class.

> You have 10 minutes to walk around the classroom.
>
> Find someone who does an activity in the grid.
>
> Fill in their name.
>
> You cannot answer the same question twice!
>
> The aim is to complete a row (diagonally, vertically or horizontally) – when you have done that, you shout 'BINGO!'

has an alarm clock	keeps a pet in their room at night	had a good night's sleep last night	takes day naps	uses their phone in bed
sleeps in at the weekend	practises relaxation exercises before bed	reads in bed	drinks tea or coffee before bed	eats a small snack before bedtime
drinks energy drinks to make up for lack of sleep	finds it difficult to get out of bed in the morning	gets 8–10 hours of sleep per night	gets the recommended 8 hours sleep per night	finds it difficult to fall asleep
goes to bed late	wakes up energised and jumps out of bed	stays up late playing online games	gets out of bed at the last minute	wakes up in the middle of the night
had a weird or funny dream last night	avoids screens for two hours before bed	has sleepwalked	falls asleep to music	gets 60 minutes of exercise per day

CLASS DISCUSSION

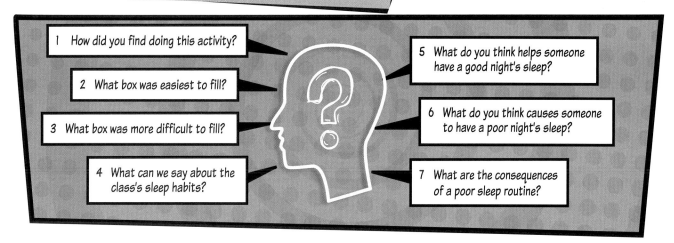

1. How did you find doing this activity?

2. What box was easiest to fill?

3. What box was more difficult to fill?

4. What can we say about the class's sleep habits?

5. What do you think helps someone have a good night's sleep?

6. What do you think causes someone to have a poor night's sleep?

7. What are the consequences of a poor sleep routine?

Teenagers and Sleep

Have you ever found that you have trouble going to bed early or you can't get out of bed in the morning? There is a biological reason for this.

During the teenage years, the body's internal 24-hour clock (also called its circadian rhythm) is reset, so teenagers fall asleep later at night and wake up earlier in the morning. The reason for this is that the brain hormone melatonin (which is responsible for making us feel sleepy) is released later in the night. This is sometimes called 'Night Owl Syndrome'.

 Go to YouTube and search for 'Why Are Teens So Sleepy?' (3:03) to watch a video about teenagers and the circadian rhythm.

 Go to YouTube and search for 'What happens when we sleep?' (2:44) by The Economist to find out how sleep works and how it affects your physical and mental health.

Sleep and Screen Time

In the sleep-walking bingo activity, we looked at whether your classmates use phones and devices before bed.

Staying up late on phones or gaming devices can affect your sleep schedule and your quality of sleep because the light from electrical devices delays the release of melatonin and tricks your brain into thinking it's time to stay awake, even when you want to go to sleep. You should turn off all electrical devices about two hours before going to sleep. It's probably best to leave your phone in another room so you are not tempted to look at it. And the answer to your question? Use an alarm clock!

Relaxation Exercises and Sleep

Performing relaxation techniques before going to bed is a great way to help you fall asleep quicker and get a good night's sleep.

Go to YouTube and search for 'Five Minute Mindful Breathing' (5:00) by Epworth HealthCare to learn a breathing technique that helps you drift off to sleep.

If you are still awake after 20 minutes, get out of bed and do something like read a book or drink a glass of water, then get back to bed.

Write down what is worrying you and set it aside to deal with the next day.

Ten Tips for a Good Night's Sleep

Tip 1: Stick to the same routine – get up and go to bed at the same time each morning and night. Stick to the routine at the weekends.

Tip 2: If you are taking naps, take them early in the afternoon and limit them to 30 minutes.

Tip 3: Turn off all electronic devices about two hours before going to bed.

Tip 4: Create a room that is comfortable to sleep in. If possible, it should be cool, dark and quiet.

Tip 5: Avoid going to bed hungry or too full. Eat a small snack before going to bed. A full stomach or an empty one can keep you awake.

Tip 6: Do something calming before going to bed such as having a bath, reading a book, listening to music or doing relaxation exercises.

Tip 7: Get the recommended 60 minutes of exercise per day. This helps to promote sleep.

Tip 8: Try to sort out your worries before you go to bed. If something is troubling you, write it down on a piece of paper and set it aside to deal with the next day.

Tip 9: Placing lavender drops on your pillow can help you relax and fall asleep easier.

Tip 10: If you are still finding it difficult to fall asleep, concentrate on your breathing. Count each inhale and exhale, or try counting sheep.

REFLECTION ON MY LEARNING
Track Your Sleep

Use the chart below to track if you are getting the recommended amount of sleep in the week. There are also watches and apps that can help you keep track of your sleep. Bring the tracker to class next week to compare your results with your classmates and brainstorm ideas on how to improve your sleep.

	MONDAY	TUESDAY	WEDNESDAY	THURSDAY	FRIDAY	SATURDAY	SUNDAY
Time I woke up							
Time I fell asleep							
Hours slept							
What I did before going to bed							
Physical activity							
How I felt during the day							

What did you learn about your sleep routine from completing this tracker?

_____

_____

1. If you are **not** getting the recommended amount of sleep per night, think of what you can do to improve this.

_____

_____

2. A small change I could make to improve my sleep routine is:

_____

_____

3. The reason for this is:

_____

_____

4. I feel this would help because:

_____

_____

1. If you **are** getting the recommended amount of sleep per night – well done! Think about what habits or activities could help you maintain this.

_____

_____

2. A habit or activity that has helped me maintain a good sleep routine is:

_____

_____

3. I find this helpful because:

_____

LESSON 31

The Effects of Alcohol

Learning Outcome: 2.5

responsible · connected · aware

By the end of this lesson, you will:

→ understand how alcohol affects personal health, wellbeing and relationships

→ demonstrate the skills to resist the pressure to drink alcohol.

KEYWORDS

Standard drink

Alcohol limit

ADDITIONAL RESOURCES

www.drugs.ie Provides drug and alcohol information and support.

www.drinkaware.ie Provides facts on alcohol use in Ireland.

www.barnardos.ie/resources/young-people/drugs-alcohol Provides support and resources for young people experiencing issues with alcohol themselves or in the home.

www.askaboutalcohol.ie Provides support and advice on alcohol use for individuals or families experiencing alcohol issues.

Alcohol plays a very big part in Irish culture and social life. We are exposed to alcohol from many different angles: through TV adverts, sport sponsorship or generally accepted ideas on the role of alcohol in any type of social situation, from baptisms to funerals.

INDIVIDUAL ACTIVITY

Read these statements and tick which ones are myths, which ones are facts, and which ones you are unsure of. Discuss the statements as a class afterwards.

Statement	Myth	Fact	Unsure
1. Alcohol works to cheer people up.			
2. Drinking coffee or taking a cold shower after drinking helps sober a person up.			
3. Mixing alcohol with energy drinks is potentially dangerous.			
4. It is OK to have one drink and drive.			
5. In Ireland, it is against the law to sell alcohol to anyone under 18.			
6. Alcohol use can lead to risky behaviour.			
7. If a person starts drinking at age 15, they are four times more likely to have issues with alcohol dependency.			
8. Binge drinking is defined as drinking six or more standard drinks in one sitting (i.e. three or more pints of beer, six or more pub measures of spirits or 600ml or more of wine).			
9. Too much alcohol can poison a person's body.			
10. Drinking alcohol can make a person a risk to others› safety.			
11. Eating while drinking slows down the absorption of alcohol.			
12. Women and men can drink the same amount of alcohol, with the same effects.			

Facts About Alcohol

Alcohol increases the risk of road accidents

Alcohol is involved in two in every five fatal road collisions. A person who drinks and drives does not just put themselves at risk but also their passengers, other drivers and road-users, and pedestrians. The introduction of random breath testing and the lowering of the drink-driving limits have improved road safety. The Road Safety Authority's advice is **never ever drink and drive**.

Drinking alcohol during adolescence can damage the developing teenage brain

The human brain continues to develop during adolescence and is not considered fully developed until a person reaches their mid-twenties. This means that during adolescence, the brain is much more at risk to damage from alcohol. Drinking alcohol while the brain is still developing damages two key parts of the brain: the part responsible for logic, reasoning, self-regulation and judgement, and the part responsible for learning and memory. This damage can be long term and irreversible.

Alcohol can cause mental health problems

Alcohol is a depressant. After drinking alcohol, a person can feel low or down. In the long term, alcohol use can cause depression, anxiety and stress. Drinking alcohol can prevent young people developing the coping skills and resilience that contribute to positive mental health in later life. As well as that, when a person drinks too much, they can lose their inhibitions, which can greatly increase the chances of them getting into embarrassing situations at best, or risky or dangerous situations at worst. All these factors can seriously impact on a young person's mental health.

 Alcohol affects sports performance

If you are serious about athletics or playing sports, then alcohol is a no-go area. Alcohol affects endurance, muscle development and recovery. It affects the ability of muscles to absorb the nutrients they need to work properly. Playing sports with a hangover increases the risk of cramp and affects coordination, reaction time and balance. Alcohol can also reduce B vitamins, which help repair the body after injury, and testosterone in males, which is needed for muscle development.

GLASS OF PROSECCO
12% (150ml)
114 calories
2 grams sugar
Half teaspoon

CAN OF CIDER
4.5% (500ml x 6 pack)
1,260 calories
126 grams sugar
25 teaspoons

BOTTLE OF WHITE WINE
12.5% (750ml)
564 calories
22.5 grams sugar
4.5 teaspoons

SPIRIT AND SOFT DRINK
35.5ml (of spirits)
163 calories
21 grams sugar
4 teaspoons

ALCOPOP
4% (250ml x 4 pack)
527 calories
88 grams sugar
18 teaspoons

BOTTLE OF WHITE WINE
14% (750ml)
720 calories
44 grams sugar
9 teaspoons

PINT OF LAGER
3% (568ml)
91 calories
3 grams sugar
Half teaspoon

BOTTLE OF RED WINE
12.5% (750ml)
570 calories
11 grams sugar
2 teaspoons

QUARTER BOTTLE OF WHITE WINE
12.5% (187.5ml)
141 calories
6 grams sugar
1 teaspoon

IRISH CREAM LIQUEUR
17% (50ml)
18 calories
10 grams sugar
2 teaspoons

 Starting drinking early in life increases your risk of becoming dependent

Evidence shows that young people who start drinking in their early teens are more likely to become addicted.

 **Drinking alcohol can lead to obesity**

Alcohol is high in calories and contains a lot of sugar. These calories are known as 'empty calories' because they have no nutritional value. One standard drink can contain over 200 calories. As well as that, drinking alcohol gives a false appetite, which contributes to poor eating choices, for example getting a takeaway after a night out.

 Drinking while pregnant affects the unborn child

Drinking alcohol while pregnant can affect the foetus with a range of conditions known as foetal alcohol spectrum disorder, including reduced birth weight and hearing and sight issues. Even moderate drinking increases the risk of miscarriage or stillbirth. Women are also advised not to drink if breastfeeding their baby.

Problem Drinking in the Home

Many young people in Ireland are affected by the drinking habits of their parents/guardians. It can be a big worry for a young person if a parent or guardian is drinking too much. It is important to remember the 'Seven Cs' in realising that problem drinking is not the fault of the child.

- You didn't cause it.
- You cannot cure it.
- You cannot control it.
- You can care for yourself.
- You can communicate your feelings.
- You can make healthy choices.
- You can celebrate yourself.

(*Source: www.barnardos.ie*)

If you are affected by another person's drinking, it is important to talk to a trusted adult. This could be someone in your family like an aunt, uncle or grandparent. You could also talk to someone outside your family, for example a school counsellor. The 'how to get help' section of these websites can provide you with details of support services: **www.barnardos.ie/teenhelp** and **www.askaboutalcohol.ie**.

Standard Drinks and Binge Drinking

A 'standard drink' is a measure of alcohol, and how it is measured out depends on the strength of the alcohol (shown on the label as alcohol by volume or % ABV – so, for example, 5% ABV means 5 parts alcohol to 95 parts water). Binge drinking is when six or more standard drinks are consumed in one sitting (for example, three pints of 4.5% beer).

Drinks should be spaced out over the week and should never be saved up to drink on one occasion. The low-risk drinking guidelines displayed in the infographic are for adults only (there is no safe limit of drinking for anyone drinking illegally under the age of 18), but it is important to note that health authorities now advise that there is no 'safe' level of alcohol intake regardless of whether the person drinking is an adult or an adolescent. The advice of public health experts in Ireland to young people is not to drink alcohol, or to delay the age of starting to drink alcohol for as long as possible.

A STANDARD DRINK IS

Half pint of lager, beer or stout (284ml) — Small glass of wine (100ml) — Pub measure of spirit (35.5ml)

Low-risk drinking guidelines

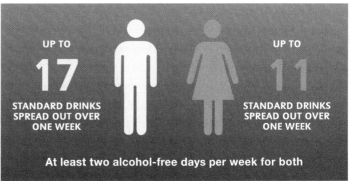

UP TO **17** STANDARD DRINKS SPREAD OUT OVER ONE WEEK

UP TO **11** STANDARD DRINKS SPREAD OUT OVER ONE WEEK

At least two alcohol-free days per week for both

How Alcohol Affects Different Parts of the Body

The moment alcohol enters your system, it starts affecting your body and mind. Alcohol passes through the body from the mouth to the stomach into the circulatory system, the brain, the kidneys, lungs and liver.

Brain

Alcohol affects the part of the brain that is responsible for self-control. As a person drinks, their reactions, vision and judgement become impaired. The more a person drinks, the harder basic tasks – such as walking and talking – become. After drinking, people sometimes behave out of character, doing things they don't mean to or wouldn't if they were sober. An excessive amount of alcohol in the body can result in coma, brain damage and even death.

Eyes

Drinking too much alcohol can affect vision. Things can become blurry, or the person may start seeing double. Alcohol can irritate the blood vessels on the surface of the eyes, making them appear red and 'bloodshot'. It can also cause irritated dry eyes.

Skin

Drinking alcohol dehydrates the skin, causing puffiness and dark circles under the eyes. Alcohol can also cause water retention, which makes the face look bloated and puffy.

Speech

Too much alcohol can affect the way a person speaks, as well as what they say. It can cause slurred speech. It can also cause people to say things they wouldn't normally.

Heart

When alcohol enters the bloodstream, it can increase the heart rate and cause the blood vessels to widen, which causes flushed skin and a feeling of warmth. Drinking too much alcohol over time can damage the heart and cause heart disease.

Liver

The liver is where alcohol is broken down, but it can only deal with one drink per hour. Drinking a lot of alcohol over time can damage the liver cells, leading to a condition called cirrhosis. Most people don't know they have cirrhosis until it is too late.

Kidneys

Alcohol stimulates urine production, which causes frequent trips to the bathroom. This can lead to dehydration.

Reproductive organs

Drinking too much alcohol over time can cause infertility in men and women.

Stomach

Alcohol enters the stomach first. If the stomach is empty, the alcohol passes straight through into the intestines; if the stomach has food in it, the alcohol is absorbed more slowly. Alcohol stimulates the stomach juices, which causes an increased appetite. Drinking too much alcohol over time can cause ulcers.

Go to YouTube and search for 'The Journey of Alcohol Through the Body' (4:09) by HSE Health and Wellbeing. Watch the video to learn how alcohol affects your organs.

REFLECTION ON MY LEARNING

From what you learned in today's lesson, design a t-shirt with a slogan or graphic that would encourage young people not to drink or to delay their decision to drink alcohol.

LESSON 32

The Effects of Smoking

Learning Outcome: 2.5

responsible   aware

By the end of this lesson, you will:

➡ have considered the health and social effects of smoking

➡ have explored different techniques that help you resist the pressure to smoke.

KEYWORDS

Lung cancer

Cardiovascular disease

ADDITIONAL RESOURCES

www.quit.ie Dedicated to raising awareness about the dangers of smoking and provides advice and help for how to quit.

www.ash.ie Provides information about the dangers of smoking and e-cigarettes.

INDIVIDUAL ACTIVITY

Read this magazine article about smoking and answer the questions that follow.

How Smart is it to Smoke?

Answer: Not very!

The fact of the matter is, smoking is stupid. Plain and simple.

When you think of the physical action of what you are doing, it's pretty ridiculous, not to mention foul. You are taking smoky air into your lungs and then blowing it out. Would you run a tube up a smoky chimney and do the same? Would you stand right behind a bus and inhale the fumes? No!

It's not like anyone sets out to be a smoker. Sometimes it's curiosity, sometimes it's boredom, sometimes it's because all your friends are doing it. However, before you know what's happening, you're not just taking a cigarette from someone else, you're trying to buy a packet, or asking someone to buy you some (and think of the cost of them – over €16 a pack!). Now it's not just when you're with your mates, it's when your parents aren't home and you're having a cheeky puff out the window. Next thing you know, you're craving another, you're addicted, and you're not even sure how much you like them.

A smoker is someone who smokes, and it doesn't have to be twenty a day. And being called a smoker is no compliment.

'How do I look?'

Before we even get started on the health risks, there are other smoking concerns to consider. Your physical appearance, for example. For a start, your teeth will turn a dull beige and eventually develop brown stains starting at the gums. Lovely!

SMOKING STINKS

AND MINORS CAN LOSE THEIR LICENSE.

And not only that, your breath stinks. And we are not talking smoky-stinky, we're talking actual bad breath. Think of getting ready to go out, brushing your teeth, putting on some nice clean clothes, doing your hair – and out the door, only to light up a cigarette.

You might as well have not bothered. Hair, clothes, fingers … why waste your time getting ready when you're just going to ruin it by smelling awful? (And by the way, you might not be able to smell the cigarettes off yourself, but as soon as anyone else is around you after you've smoked, it's the first thing they'll smell, and it's gross.)

And if stinking to high heavens isn't bad enough, smoking actually causes premature ageing of the skin too. Now you may think this is no cause for concern right now, but you'll soon know all about it. Not only will it give you wrinkles around your eyes and forehead, you'll also get lovely wrinkles – 'smoker's lines', they're called – around your mouth. So while your non-smoking mates are enjoying getting ID'd by bouncers at the age of 28 ('Really? I look underage?'), you're getting asked for your pensioner's travel pass on the bus. Not good.

'What about my health?'

If brown teeth, stinky breath and premature wrinkles aren't enough to put you off smoking, then maybe the fact that it's the number one cause of lung cancer might convince you … not to mention the fact that your life will be shortened by ten to fifteen years, not to mention the yellow, sticky tar building up around your lungs, emphysema, bronchitis, strokes, heart disease, diabetes, cataracts … and not to mention the fact that if you were to buy one pack of cigarettes every week in Ireland for a year, you'd spend (lose) €832 annually. What a waste of money for something that not only is of absolutely zero physical benefit, but actually actively harms you physically and socially. Doesn't really seem worth it.

215

1. 'Although young people are informed about the effects of smoking, they still do not regard it as dangerous.' Do you agree with this statement? Give reasons for your answer.

   _____

   _____

2. If you were trying to reduce smoking among young people in Ireland, what three facts about smoking would you consider the most important?

   (a) _____

   (b) _____

   (c) _____

3. What is your school's policy on smoking?

   _____

   _____

4. What do you think when you see anti-smoking campaigns, either on television or on billboards? Do you think they have any impact on a person's decision to smoke?

   _____

   _____

5. Write a health warning on this box of cigarettes that you think would encourage young people to quit smoking.

What Causes the Damage?

Tobacco is a toxic substance that contains the highly addictive substance nicotine. Along with tobacco, cigarettes contain around 4,000 chemicals, including arsenic (which is also used in rat poison) and acetone (also used in nail polish remover). Many of these are known to cause cancer.

What About Passive Smoking?

Passive smoking means breathing in other people's unfiltered exhaled smoke. This is called second-hand smoke. People who breathe in second-hand smoke are at increased risk of smoking related diseases such as cancer and heart disease. Opening a window when you smoke does not make a difference. More than 80% of smoke is invisible – you cannot see where it goes or control it. Due to the harmful effects of second-hand smoke, the Irish government introduced laws that ban smoking in indoor workplaces, including offices, restaurants, pubs and other public areas and cars where children are present.

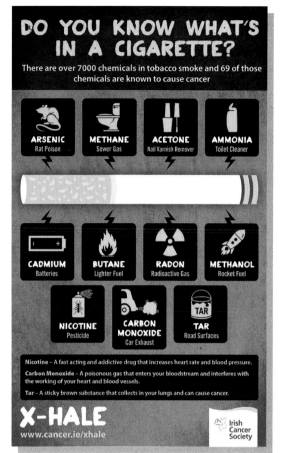

(Source: www.cancer.ie)

Some Facts About Smoking

- Smoking is the single biggest killer of people in Ireland, accounting for some 6,000 deaths every year.
- Every 6.5 seconds, someone in the world dies because of their tobacco use.
- Every cigarette a person smokes reduces their life by 11 minutes.
- One in two smokers will die from a tobacco-related illness such as cancer, heart disease, lung disease, cardiovascular disease and exacerbation of diabetes.
- One cigar can contain as much tobacco as a pack of cigarettes.
- Smoking does not relax you – it triggers stress.
- It takes 20 minutes for a smoker's pulse rate to return to normal after having a cigarette.
- Smoking can affect a person's physical fitness. Muscles need oxygen to perform and the carbon monoxide in cigarettes deprives the muscles of oxygen and causes shortness of breath.
- Smoking while pregnant damages the unborn child. It can cause low birth weight and it increases the risk of premature birth or dying after birth.
- Most smokers (83%) regret that they ever started smoking.
- Smoking 20 cigarettes a day could cost a person over €4,300 a year.
- It is illegal for anyone under the age of eighteen to buy cigarettes in Ireland.
- Young people most commonly start smoking because their friends smoke.
- The benefits of quitting smoking are felt almost immediately by the body.

I will never smoke because _____.

Go to YouTube and search for 'Smokefree Campaign Advert - Tobacco Control Smoke Free House' (0:30). Watch the video.

Dangers of Smoking Crossword

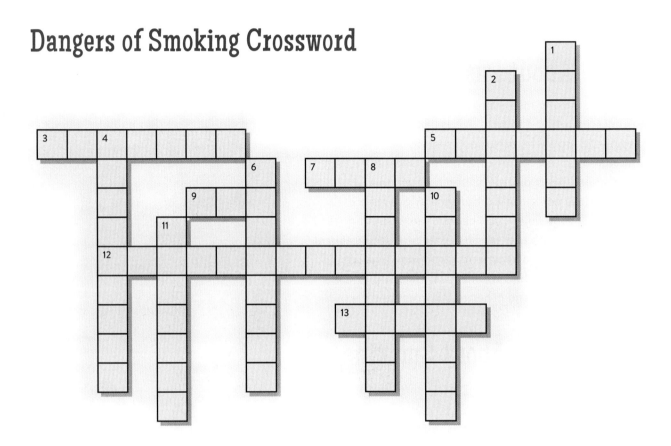

Across

3 The feeling a person gets that makes them want to smoke another cigarette.

5 One of the 7,000 chemicals used in cigarettes, also used in rat poison.

7 Cancer caused by smoking.

9 Sticky, yellow substance that builds up in the lungs.

12 Gas that robs the body of oxygen and causes shortness of breath.

13 Out of 100 people who smoke, the number of people who will die of a smoking-related illness.

Down

1 The number of minutes it takes for a smoker's heart to return to normal after smoking a cigarette.

2 This type of smoking harms non-smokers.

4 The reason why people find it is hard to give up smoking.

6 Visible signs of premature ageing caused by smoking.

8 The main addictive ingredient in cigarettes.

10 The benefits of this are felt almost immediately by the body.

11 The most common reason why young people start smoking.

(Source: www.cancer.ie)

REFLECTION ON MY LEARNING

Three things I have learned in this lesson are:

1. _____

_____

2. _____

_____

3. _____

_____

LESSON 33
Vaping

Learning Outcomes: 2.2, 2.3, 2.4, 2.5, 2.6

responsible   aware

By the end of this lesson, you will:

↠ understand what vaping is

↠ recognise the risks of vaping

↠ appreciate that vapes can damage our environment

↠ use assertive skills to resist the pressure to vape.

KEYWORDS

Vaping

Nicotine

Vape waste

ADDITIONAL RESOURCES

www2.hse.ie/living-well/quit-smoking/vaping Provides information on the risks of vaping to young people.

You have probably heard of vaping or e-cigarettes. You may have seen people vaping in public, in school, in your homes. You may even have thought about trying vaping yourself, out of curiosity or peer influence.

Some people believe that vaping is no big deal and carries no health risks. The truth is, vaping carries very real health consequences. In this lesson, we will explore what vaping is and the risks associated with it.

What is Vaping?

Vaping is the act of inhaling vapour through an e-cigarette or vape pen. It works by converting a liquid (which contains nicotine) and flavourings (which are toxic) in a cartridge to a vapour. Puffing on the vape activates a battery, which heats the liquid and in turn produces a vapour that is inhaled.

The fact that vapes come in different flavours makes it hard for young people to believe they are unsafe. These vapes were created to offer an alternative to smoking cigarettes, but now an increasing number of young people who have never smoked before are vaping. As well as containing toxic chemicals, vapes deliver the same highly addictive chemical that is in cigarettes – nicotine.

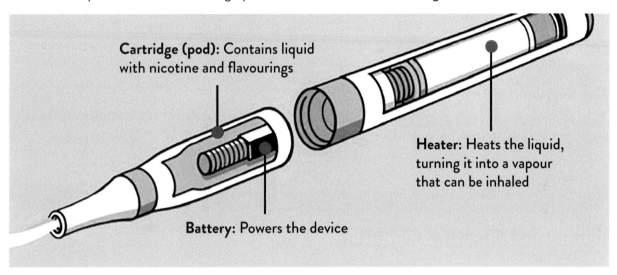

Cartridge (pod): Contains liquid with nicotine and flavourings

Heater: Heats the liquid, turning it into a vapour that can be inhaled

Battery: Powers the device

Vaping and the Law

Vaping and e-cigarettes come under the same law as smoking. This law says that it is illegal to sell any tobacco and nicotine products to someone under 18. It is also illegal for someone else to buy them for you if you are under 18.

The findings from the European Schools Project on Alcohol and other drugs (ESPAD), published by the Tobacco Free Research Institute in 2020, reported a 50% rise in e-cigarette current use in adolescents aged 16–17 years since the previous study in 2015. Nearly 4 in 10 (39%) adolescents have tried vaping, and 1 in 5 (18%) were found to be current users.

Teenagers who used e-cigarettes at some point are 50% more likely to smoke.

In 2015, 23% of 15–16-year-old Irish teenagers said they used e-cigarettes at some point. This increased to 37% in 2019. What do you think the percentage is now?

Vaping: The Risks

Despite their popularity, vapes and e-cigarettes are not harmless. They deliver a number of risks and unknowns, especially for teens.

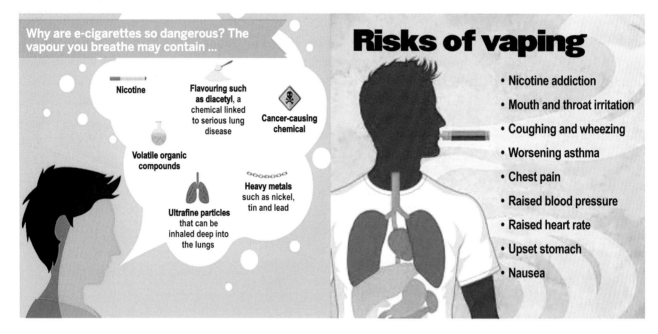

Why are e-cigarettes so dangerous? The vapour you breathe may contain ...

Nicotine

Flavouring such as diacetyl, a chemical linked to serious lung disease

Cancer-causing chemical

Volatile organic compounds

Heavy metals such as nickel, tin and lead

Ultrafine particles that can be inhaled deep into the lungs

Risks of vaping

- Nicotine addiction
- Mouth and throat irritation
- Coughing and wheezing
- Worsening asthma
- Chest pain
- Raised blood pressure
- Raised heart rate
- Upset stomach
- Nausea

Vaping and Nicotine Addiction

Teenagers' brains are still developing, so they are especially susceptible to the addictive effects of **nicotine**.

One vape cartridge could contain the same amount of **nicotine** as a whole packet of cigarettes.

Inhaling **nicotine** triggers the release of dopamine, a brain chemical that causes addiction.

Vaping is expensive! Your money could be better spent on things you enjoy doing.

The liquid inside vapes contains **nicotine**, which is a highly addictive drug.

Nicotine can cause long-term damage to a young person's brain, affecting memory, concentration and learning ability.

People who become addicted to **nicotine** feel irritable if they need to vape, have trouble concentrating or sleeping, find it difficult to stop even though they may know it is bad for them.

Vaping 'just a little' can be a gateway to addiction in young people.

Nicotine causes withdrawal symptoms such as irritability, headaches, restlessness, decreased or increased appetite and mood swings.

Vape Waste and the Environment

Vape waste is the waste associated with vapes, including disposable vape pens, pods, cartridges, e-liquid containers, packaging and batteries. Vapes are being thrown away carelessly instead of being recycled and this has a very harmful effect on the environment:

- **Plastic waste:** The pod is made from plastic, which takes hundreds of years to decompose.

- **Hazardous waste:** The nicotine and chemicals in the vapes can leak into the environment, polluting rivers and oceans or being eaten by wildlife and pets.

- **Electronic waste:** Vapes contain lithium batteries and heating elements. As they decompose, they release toxic chemicals into the environment.

What Young People are Saying

The following quotes are from young people who took part in a study called 'E-cigarette and smoking use among adolescents in Ireland: 2020. A Focus Group Study'.

Read each quote and discuss with your partners whether you think they are true, sometimes true or false.

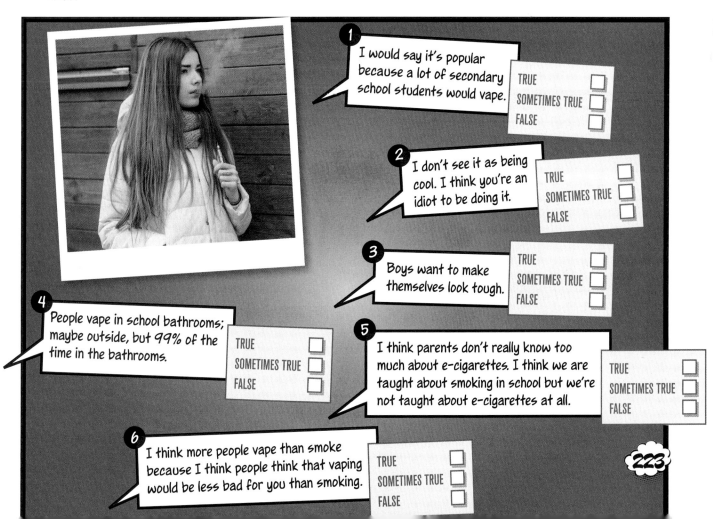

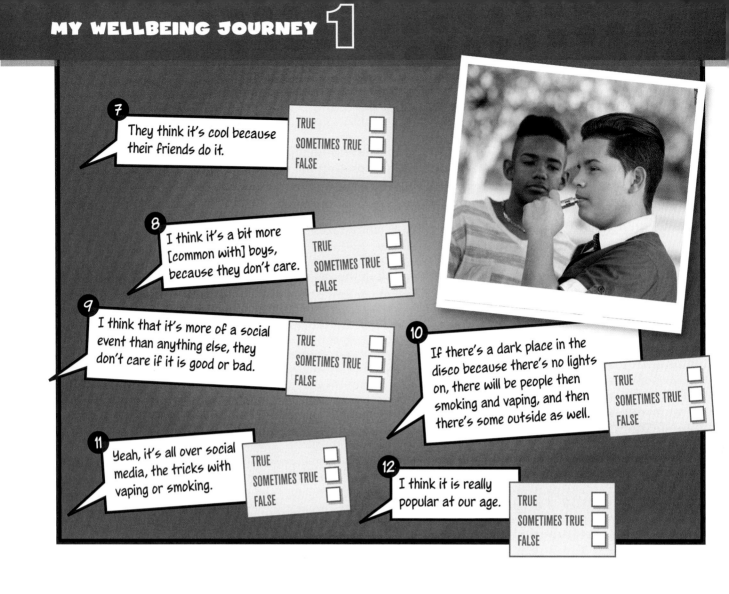

7 They think it's cool because their friends do it.

TRUE ☐
SOMETIMES TRUE ☐
FALSE ☐

8 I think it's a bit more [common with] boys, because they don't care.

TRUE ☐
SOMETIMES TRUE ☐
FALSE ☐

9 I think that it's more of a social event than anything else, they don't care if it is good or bad.

TRUE ☐
SOMETIMES TRUE ☐
FALSE ☐

10 If there's a dark place in the disco because there's no lights on, there will be people then smoking and vaping, and then there's some outside as well.

TRUE ☐
SOMETIMES TRUE ☐
FALSE ☐

11 Yeah, it's all over social media, the tricks with vaping or smoking.

TRUE ☐
SOMETIMES TRUE ☐
FALSE ☐

12 I think it is really popular at our age.

TRUE ☐
SOMETIMES TRUE ☐
FALSE ☐

CLASS DISCUSSION

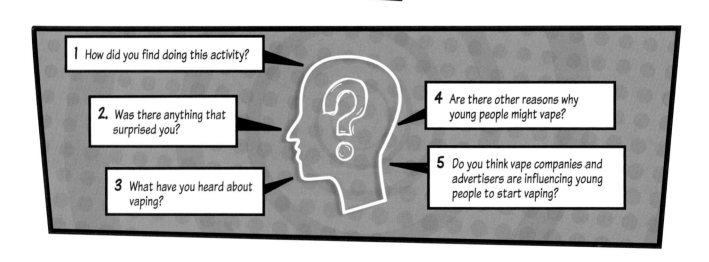

1 How did you find doing this activity?

2. Was there anything that surprised you?

3 What have you heard about vaping?

4 Are there other reasons why young people might vape?

5 Do you think vape companies and advertisers are influencing young people to start vaping?

Resisting the Pressure to Vape

It is important to realise that the vast majority of teenagers have no interest in vaping. It is important that you feel comfortable saying 'no' to people who put pressure on you to vape. What would you do if someone encourages you to vape? Here are some tips to deal with the pressure.

Know your own mind. If you don't want to vape, you don't have to. Just because your friends do it, it doesn't mean it's right for you.

Feel comfortable saying 'no'. A good friend will accept a 'no' and won't pressure you into doing something.

Talk to a trusted adult. If you feel pressured to vape, it is a good idea to seek advice from an adult.

Plan ahead. Have a statement ready to resist vaping: 'Vaping is stupid – it's bad for your health and the environment'. 'My sport is too important to me'.

You don't need an excuse. If you don't want to do something, it's your right to say no.

Use short, clear statements. 'I don't think it's healthy'. 'I don't want to'.

REFLECTION ON MY LEARNING

Raising Awareness

You have been tasked with raising awareness with young people about the health risks of vaping. You can do this by creating a poster, slideshow, advertisement or infographic (www.canva.com).

Your poster, slideshow or infographic should include:

- A catchy slogan to grab your audience's attention
- Images or text that will appeal to young people
- Facts and information you think will persuade young people not to vape (e.g. addiction, health risks, environmental risks)
- Advice on how to resist the pressure to vape
- Any other information you think is relevant.

Assessment: CBAs in SPHE

The focus of assessment in SPHE is to allow you to demonstrate the knowledge, skills, dispositions and values you have gained through your SPHE classes. Over the course of the three years of Junior Cycle, you will engage in one Classroom-Based Assessment (CBA) in SPHE. You have a choice of a Portfolio or Action project:

Title	Format	Student preparation
Portfolio of my learning and reflection in SPHE	Individual selection of items of work, such as: - digital - written texts - posters - audio-visual - multi-modal	Students will choose three pieces of work, completed over time and linked to different strands of learning within the course, and present these accompanied by a reflection on why each piece was chosen and how it marked important learning for the student in SPHE.
OR		
Taking action for SPHE	- Individual or small group project - Can be presented in a wide range of formats	Students will, over a specified time, with support and guidance from the teacher, research, report and reflect on an action they have taken to raise awareness about or promote an aspect of health/wellbeing studied in the SPHE short course.

While you cannot complete your SPHE CBA in 1st Year, you can certainly start to develop the skills and experiences required now. You might like to try some of the suggested projects described below.

Unit 1: Understanding Myself and Others

TAKING ACTION FOR SPHE

Supporting the Wellbeing of 1st Years

Learning Outcomes: 1.3, 1.4, 1.6, 1.8, 2.1, 3.1, 3.2, 3.4, 4.4

Take action and create a plan that would help your school support the wellbeing of 1st Years and ensure your school is an inclusive place where everyone feels respected and valued.

Ideas for your plan

Create a survey which will determine:

● What the school are already doing well to support 1st Years and their wellbeing

● What students think would further support their wellbeing and time in 1st Year, including any improvements that could be made

● What the students and school management could do to make your school an inclusive place, where everyone feels respected and valued.

Using your survey results, compile a report for the Student Council of suggested recommendations for changes. Request they discuss it at their next meeting and bring it to the attention of the school management.

Unit 2: Anti-Bullying

PORTFOLIO ITEM

A Resource to Take a Stand Against Bullying

Learning Outcomes: 1.8, 2.7, 2.8, 2.10

Create a resource that gives advice and support on how to deal with and stand up to bullying and abusive behaviour both online and offline.

Your resource can include:

- Definition of bullying and cyberbullying
- Bullying/cyberbullying survey
- Examples of bullying and abusive behaviour online and offline
- Practical tips and advice and suggested actions to take if you experience bullying, cyberbullying or online abusive behaviours
- Organisations and people that can provide support and help
- Advice and tips on how to be an upstander and how to safely report and support targets of online abuse
- Anything else you think is important to support others.

Your resource could be presented as a video, leaflet, poster or slideshow. The choice is yours!

Unit 3: Respectful Communication Online and Offline

PORTFOLIO ITEM

Cartoon Strip or Script on Effective Communication and Listening Skills

Learning Outcomes: 1.7, 1.8

Create a cartoon strip or a script for a drama or TV show that demonstrates a scenario where effective communication and listening skills are demonstrated.

In your cartoon strip or script, include:

- Text to explain the situation

- Speech bubbles which demonstrate effective communication and listening skills

- Hints on body language and tone that will aid actors to demonstrate effective and respectful communication skills.

227

Unit 4: Relationships and Sexuality

PORTFOLIO ITEM

A Report on Gendered Advertising

Learning Outcomes: 1.4, 1.5, 1.6, 3.6

Working in groups of three or four, choose three advertisements that are aimed at young people to see if they use gender stereotypes to sell their products or services. You can choose advertisements that you see on TV, in magazines or on social media (or a mix of all of these). Aim to review a mix of advertisements: those aimed at teenage boys, those aimed at teenage girls, and those aimed at all teens. Write a report on your findings, including the following elements:

- A title indicating what your report is about
- A clear structure: an introduction stating what your study is about, the types of advertisements you are examining, and where and when you saw them
- A short paragraph reporting your findings, e.g. the roles given to the people in the advertisements or the customers suggested by the marketing
- A short paragraph reviewing these findings: whether the adverts conform to and reinforce gender stereotypes or whether they are more 'gender neutral' (aimed at all teens rather than just one gender)
- A paragraph stating any recommendations or advice for marketing companies to help them avoid reinforcing gender stereotypes.

Unit 5: Emotional Wellbeing

PORTFOLIO ITEM

Booklet to Promote Wellbeing

Learning Outcomes: 4.1, 4.3, 4.4, 4.9

Create a physical or digital booklet (you can use **www.bookcreator.com** or **www.padlet.com**) that acts as a supportive resource in promoting a young person's wellbeing. Be as creative as you like!

You could include:

- Activities or resources that promote wellbeing, e.g.
  - positive affirmations
  - jokes
  - quotes
  - a 'mood boost' list
  - an 'acts of kindness' list
  - a collection of photos that make them happy
  - a wellbeing journal
  - a playlist
  - a list of coping strategies that could be helpful in challenging times
  - a gratitude diary.
- Information on organisations that can provide advice, help and support to young people, as well as information on the type of support they offer.

Unit 6: Healthy Choices

TAKING ACTION FOR SPHE

Awareness Campaign Promoting Healthy Choices

Learning Outcomes: 2.1, 2.2, 2.4, 2.5, 2.10

Your class will create an awareness campaign that promotes **healthy choices** among teenagers.

1. Decide what you want to raise awareness about. You can pick one of the suggestions below or come up with your own:
   ● The importance of sleep for adolescents
   ● How unhealthy foods and drinks are marketed and advertised
   ● Healthy eating ideas and tips for young people
   ● The benefits of physical activity
   ● The importance of a balanced diet
   ● The risks of vaping or using drugs and alcohol
   ● How to form healthy habits.

2. Decide on your awareness campaign slogan. Try to use rhyme, alliteration or a catchy phrase to make the slogan memorable.

3. Decide on your target audience. Is it other 1st Years or the whole school?

Your awareness campaign could include a talk, slideshow, poster, leaflet, advertisement, video, social media challenge, infographic, podcast, school blog, speech, survey or anything else you can think of. Be as creative as you like!